EVERYDAY
Spice

The heart-healthy way to make over 60 of your favourite recipes

WITHDRAWN

SIMON &
SCHUSTER
ILLUSTRATED

First published in Great Britain in 2012 by Simon & Schuster UK Ltd
A CBS COMPANY

1 3 5 7 9 10 8 6 4 2

SIMON & SCHUSTER
ILLUSTRATED BOOKS
Simon & Schuster UK Ltd
222 Gray's Inn Road
London
WC1X 8HB

www.simonandschuster.co.uk

Simon & Schuster Australia, Sydney
Simon & Schuster India, New Delhi

Commercial director: Ami Richards
Senior commissioning editor: Nicky Hill
Project editor: Salima Hirani
Designer: Geoff Fennell
BHF Senior dietitian: Victoria Taylor
Photography: William Shaw
Styling: Liz Hippisley
Food styling: Sara Lewis
Production manager: Katherine Thornton

A CIP catalogue record for this book is available from the British Library

ISBN 978-1-4711-359-8

Printed and bound in China
Colour reproduction by Dot Gradations Ltd, UK

Contents

Introduction

It is rumoured that healthy food equals bland food, but at the British Heart Foundation, we think that couldn't be further from the truth. A healthy meal has no nutritional value unless it is eaten, so it is vital that our meals are not only good for you, but that they taste good, too. But rather than relying on ingredients like salt and butter to add flavour, using herbs and spices – including chilli, if you like a little heat – allows you to make meals that taste great without having to compromise on healthy eating.

And the range of ingredients available to us has never been better. The ease with which we are able to travel abroad has enabled many of us to try new foods and, combined with the diverse range of cultures within modern Britain today, it's impossible to ignore the influence that this has had on our eating habits. As a result, hot and spicy foods, which would once have been thought of as exotic, have increasingly found their way onto our kitchen tables. And foods from as far away as Asia, Africa and the Caribbean have become commonplace within many of our diets.

But for those of you who might be more familiar with hot and spicy food, finding ways to cook traditional dishes in a more heart-healthy way, without sacrificing taste, is also important. We know that, in the UK, the risk of heart disease and stroke varies between people from different ethnic groups. So it's vital that, while we embrace all the flavours of our traditional meals, we also learn how to adapt the way we cook and eat them to make them more suitable as part of our modern lifestyles. In doing so it will help to lower cholesterol and blood pressure levels and make it easier to maintain a healthy weight, all of which will help to keep our hearts healthy in the long term.

So, whether you are looking to cook traditional dishes in a healthier way, are a lover of hot and spicy foods, or just want to try something different, there's nothing to stop you enjoying the bright and exciting flavours that spices can provide. Healthy meals that don't compromise on taste – that's the real secret to healthy eating. So don't keep it to yourself; pass it on!

Victoria Taylor

Victoria Taylor, Senior dietitian, British Heart Foundation.

Looking after your heart

If you are reading this book, chances are that you have a heart condition, or feel you are at risk of developing one. Whatever your situation, by making healthy lifestyle choices you can help to protect your heart health and reduce the risk of developing coronary heart disease (CHD), or help to prevent your heart condition from getting worse. It's never too late to change your lifestyle.

The term cardiovascular disease (CVD) refers to all diseases of the heart and circulation, including coronary heart disease (angina and heart attack), heart failure and stroke.

Coronary heart disease (CHD) is the single most common cause of death in the UK, and nearly 2.7 million people are living with CHD in the UK. CHD begins when the coronary arteries (the arteries that supply the heart muscle with oxygen-rich blood) become narrowed by a gradual build up of fatty material (known as atheroma) within their walls. This condition is known as atherosclerosis. The best way to reduce your risk of developing CHD, or to prevent any further problems if you already have CHD, is to make simple adjustments to your lifestyle and address any risk factors that may affect your heart health (see box, opposite page).

Changing your lifestyle can seem daunting, but the best way to go about making important changes to the way you live is to start small and go on from there. Select the one thing that you want to change the most, and begin there. Remember – your health is important. One in three of all deaths in the UK are due to diseases of the heart and circulatory system. You don't have to be one of them. Take action to protect your heart now.

Adjust your diet

Avoiding certain foods and including others can help to reduce your risk of developing CHD. A balanced diet combined with a healthy lifestyle will help you to maintain a healthy weight. If you are trying to lose weight, avoid faddy diets that exclude whole food groups. Instead, aim to eat regular meals (breakfast, lunch and an evening meal) and ensure your meals are balanced and that you are eating at least five portions of fruit and vegetables a day (see page 8). It might also help you to keep an eye on your portion sizes. If you find you are piling food onto your plate, try using a smaller plate, or try measuring out your portions by using a particular serving spoon or cup.

Give up smoking

This is the single most important thing you can do to improve your heart health. Within a year of stopping, your risk of heart attack is reduced by about half. If you want to quit, getting support is vital. Ask at your GP's surgery if there is a nurse or counsellor who can help, or look for a local stop-smoking service. You could also ask your doctor or pharmacist about nicotine replacement therapy (NRT) or medication that could help you to quit.

Get active!

Being physically active is good for your heart, so aim to get at least 30 minutes of moderate-intensity physical activity a day at least five days per week – walking, cycling and swimming are among activities that help protect the heart. Also, limit the time you spend in sedentary activities, such as watching TV.

Drink sensibly

If you drink alcohol, keep to recommended limits and avoid binge drinking. Women should not exceed two to three units per day and men should have no more than three or four. (One unit of alcohol is the equivalent of half a pint of beer (3.5% alcohol by volume (ABV)), a pub measure (25ml) of spirits or a 100ml glass of wine (10% ABV)). Moderate drinking – between one and two units per day – may offer some protection against CHD. But consuming more than this can lead to damage of the heart muscle, high blood pressure, stroke and some cancers. Alcohol is high in calories too, so regular consumption can lead to weight gain.

Have a health check

If you are over 40, you are entitled to a GP health check to assess your risk for developing CHD, so book an appointment today. Also, do see your GP if you suspect you have any of the risk factors mentioned here (see box, right).

RISK FACTORS FOR CHD:

- **smoking**
- **high blood pressure**
- **high blood cholesterol**
- **physical inactivity**
- **being overweight or obese**
- **having diabetes**
- **your gender** – research shows that men are more likely than women to develop CVD at an earlier age, but there are still over one million women in the UK living with CHD
- **your age** – your risk increases as you get older
- **having a family history of heart disease** – this means if your father, mother, brother or sister has or had CHD at a young age (under 65 for women, under 55 for men)
- **your ethnic background** – some risk factors appear to have a greater impact on people from certain ethnic groups. For instance, those from South Asian backgrounds tend to put on weight around their middle, increasing their risk of developing heart disease and diabetes, and people of Afro-Caribbean origin bear a higher risk of developing high blood pressure and having a stroke.

OTHER FACTORS THAT MIGHT AFFECT YOUR RISK OF DEVELOPING CHD ARE:

- **poverty** – people on lower incomes are more likely to have risk factors for CHD and are less likely to make healthy lifestyle choices
- **how you deal with stress**
- **high alcohol intake.**

Eating for a healthy heart

Healthy eating can help to reduce your risk of developing coronary heart disease. If you already have heart disease it can help to protect your heart from further problems. By eating well, you can help to maintain a healthy weight and reduce your risk of developing diabetes, high blood pressure, high cholesterol and some cancers.

Healthy eating does not mean boring food

All foods can be included in a healthy diet – you just need to get the balance right, and the Eatwell Plate shows us how to do this. You might think healthy eating is about eating everything in moderation, but this isn't strictly true. Think in terms of food groups. We need lots of foods from some food groups and less from others.

The Eatwell Plate

- Fruit & vegetables
- Bread, rice, potatoes, pasta
- Meat, fish, eggs, beans
- Food & drinks high in fat & sugar
- Milk & dairy foods

Fruits and vegetables

About a third of the foods we eat should be made up of fruits and vegetables. Aim to consume at least five portions per day – evidence shows that this is linked to a lower risk of heart disease. Also, try to eat a broad variety of fruits and vegetables, so that you can benefit from the variety of nutrients they all offer, as well as the fibre. Eating more fruits and vegetables allows less room in the diet for other foods that are high in saturated fat, salt and sugar. The fibre in them makes them filling to eat and helps to keep the digestive system healthy, too.

There are five ways in which to get your five-a-day – fruits and vegetables can be **fresh**, **frozen**, **tinned** (in juice or water), **dried** or **juiced**. Juice counts as one portion, once a day, but smoothies count as up to two portions, provided a portion contains 80g (about 3oz) of whole fruit pulp and 150ml (¼ pint) of juice. Pulses, such as kidney beans, chickpeas and haricot beans, can be included in your five a day, but only as one portion per day, however much you eat. An adult portion is 80g (about 3oz) of fresh, frozen or tinned fruits or vegetables (use a handful as a rough guide), 30g (1oz) of dried fruits or 150ml (¼ pint) of juice.

Taking dietary supplements doesn't seem to have the same health benefits as eating fruit and vegetables. A balanced diet provides all the nutrients needed to keep healthy, so most adults do not need to take supplements, although some people may be prescribed them. Nutritional supplements may seem harmless enough, but they can interfere with prescribed medications and be an unnecessary expense. If you are considering taking an over-the-counter nutritional or herbal supplement, discuss it with your doctor, practice nurse or dietitian first.

TOP TIPS TO GET YOUR FIVE-A-DAY:

- **have a glass of fruit juice when you get up**
- **sweeten porridge and cereals with dried fruit rather than sugar or honey**
- **snack on fruit or crunchy vegetable sticks rather than biscuits or crisps**
- **add some salad to your sandwiches**
- **have two portions of vegetables or salad with your evening meal**
- **end your meal with some fruit salad or stewed fruit served with yoghurt or low-fat custard.**

Milk and dairy foods

Dairy products are important as they provide protein and calcium, and also vitamins A and B12. However, it's important to be aware that the fat content varies greatly between foods in this group, and much of the fat they contain is saturated. Choosing low-fat options, such as semi-skimmed, 1% or skimmed milk and low-fat yoghurts, allows you to benefit from the nutrients in dairy products while consuming less or virtually none of the saturated fat.

As a guide, two to three portions of milk and dairy foods a day should be enough to meet the average adult's requirement for calcium. This includes milk in hot drinks and on cereal, and milk that you have as a drink as well as yoghurts and cheese.

Starchy foods

About a third of the food you eat should be made up of starchy foods, so base each of your meals around the foods in this important group. The exact quantity needed will vary from person to person, depending on how active you are. This group of foods includes breads (including chapatis and naan), rice, potatoes, pasta, couscous, yam and plantain.

Choose wholegrain or high-fibre starchy foods whenever you can, as these provide energy that is released slowly, so they will keep you going until your next meal with less temptation to snack. Foods high in soluble fibre, such as porridge, beans, lentils and nuts, may help to lower cholesterol levels.

Bread, rice and pasta have a bad reputation for being fattening, but that's only really true if you add lots of fat to them while cooking them or preparing them to eat. Bake, boil or steam starchy foods instead of frying them, and avoid adding fat once they are cooked – for example, don't add butter to mashed potatoes or chapatis, or creamy sauces to pasta or rice.

If you don't drink milk or eat any dairy foods, use a substitute, such as soya milk, with added calcium. Go for unsweetened versions.

Non-dairy sources of protein

Include lean meat, fish, eggs, beans and other non-dairy sources of protein in your diet two or three times per day – they also provide vitamins and minerals like iron. Use low- or reduced-fat versions of these foods. Remove visible fat and skin from red or white meat, and cook them without adding fat wherever possible.

Also include fish, especially oily fish, which provides omega-3 fatty acids that help to keep your heart healthy and improve the chances of survival after a heart attack. Aim to have one portion (140g/5oz) per week or two to three portions if you have had a heart attack in the past.

When it comes to eggs, bear in mind that, for most people, there is no limit recommended for eggs eaten as part of a healthy, balanced diet – good news if you are

fond of them. Use healthy cooking methods when you do have eggs – instead of frying an egg, try to boil or poach it, and avoid adding butter to scrambled eggs.

If you are vegetarian, it is important to include in your diet foods from this food group, such as beans, pulses and soya, and not to rely too heavily on dairy foods for protein. This allows you get enough iron and protein in your diet while keeping your intake of saturated fat to a minimum.

Cutting down on salt

Regularly eating too much salt is linked to raised blood pressure. The recommended maximum per day for an adult is 6g – about a teaspoon. On average, we are eating too much salt. Check food labels carefully – 75% of the salt we eat is already in our food. When buying foods, stick to products that are low in salt (containing 0.3g per 100g or less) or sodium (containing 0.1g per 100g or less). Using less salt doesn't necessarily mean less flavour. Season your dishes with herbs, spices, chilli, garlic, lemon and black pepper instead.

TOP TIPS TO CUT THE SATURATED FAT:

- **switch to low-fat milk and low-fat yoghurt**
- **use reduced-fat cheeses and grate hard cheeses** so that you use less of them
- **remove the visible fat and skin from both red meat and poultry**
- **use healthier cooking methods to cut down on the fat you add to foods during cooking**
- **use unsaturated fats, such as rapeseed, olive, sunflower or corn oils and unsaturated spreads**
- **swap snacks such as cakes, biscuits and chocolate for healthier options** – for instance, fruit, low-fat yoghurts and unsalted nuts and seeds.

STORE-CUPBOARD ESSENTIALS

Keeping a well-stocked kitchen will help you to cook healthy meals from scratch with minimum effort. You don't need fancy or expensive ingredients – just the basics and a few extras will equip you well. The items listed on this page include many store-cupboard staples that will help you to prepare the recipes in this book, along with others that are useful to have in as they provide you with all you need to prepare a broad variety of healthy meals. Some of our spicy dishes use unusual ingredients, and sources of these are suggested on pages 12–13. And don't forget to keep your kitchen stocked up with a good variety of fruits and vegetables to help you and your family towards consuming your five-a-day.

In the fridge:
- **low-fat milk** (semi-skimmed, 1% or skimmed)
- **low-fat natural yoghurt**
- **eggs**
- **unsaturated fat spread**
- **unsweetened orange juice**
- **tofu**
- **reduced-fat mayonnaise**
- **fresh red and green finger chillies, Scotch bonnet peppers**
- **fresh root ginger**
- **lemons and limes**.

In the freezer:
- **wholegrain breads** – sliced loaves, pitta bread and Indian flatbreads, rolls, wraps
- **filo pastry**
- **oily fish** – salmon, sardines, mackerel
- **lean meat** – chicken, turkey, lean red meat

- **vegetables** – mixed vegetables, peas, sweetcorn, broad beans.

In the store cupboard:
- **tinned or dried beans and pulses** – chickpeas, lentils, kidney beans, pigeon peas and black eye beans
- **tinned fruit in juice**
- **wholewheat pasta and noodles**
- **wholemeal flour, plain flour, cornflour**
- **rice** – white and brown Basmati, long-grain white rice
- **couscous**
- **dried fruit** – raisins, sultanas, dried apricots
- **unsalted seeds and nuts** – sesame, sunflower, almonds, peanuts
- **low-salt stock cubes**
- **fresh garlic**
- **herbs and spices** – mixed spice, cinnamon, cloves, nutmeg, mustard seeds, fenugreek leaves, bay leaves, cardamom pods, curry powder, black pepper, cayenne pepper, ajowan seeds, panch phoran, asafoetida, chilli powder, cumin, coriander, cumin-coriander powder, curry leaves, garam masala, turmeric, paprika, oregano seeds, chilli flakes
- **tomato purée**
- **vinegars** – balsamic, white wine
- **sugar** – brown and caster
- **unsaturated oils** like rapeseed and sunflower oil
- **honey**
- **mustard oil**
- **reduced-sodium soy sauce**
- **sweet chilli sauce**
- **bicarbonate of soda**
- **tinned fish in water or unsaturated oil** – sardines, salmon.

On the window sill or in the garden:
- **thyme**
- **coriander**
- **parsley**.

Notes on using this book

Using the recipe nutritional information

Food labels that use the traffic-light colours on their front-of-pack nutritional information make it easy for shoppers to tell at a glance whether the product is high, medium or low in fat, saturated fat, salt and sugar. We have used the same type of system for each recipe in this cookbook (in a special box at the bottom of each page, as shown below), so you can see exactly what it contains.

The 'traffic light' signposting lets you see immediately if a dish has high (red), medium (amber) or low (green) amounts of fat, saturated fat, sugars and salt per 100g (3½oz) of the food. Choose mainly greens (especially for saturated fat and salt), a few ambers and just one or two reds.

We also tell you the amount of fat, saturated fat, sugars and salt contained in one portion of each dish, and how much of the guideline daily amount (or the GDA) of those nutrients a portion of the dish will deliver. These are based on the dietary recommendations for adults of a healthy weight and average activity level. Men and women have slightly different GDAs but, to simplify, the GDA for women is used.

The nutritional analysis of the single portions is based on the number of people the recipe caters for. If a recipe serves four to six people, the nutritional analysis is based on the larger number of servings of that range (i.e. the analysis per portion is based on 6 portions).

Ingredients listed as optional or as serving options in the method have not been included in the analysis.

Chillies

Chillies appear in this book in various forms: fresh red or green chillies, fiery Scotch bonnet peppers, chilli sauce, Sichuan pepper, chilli powder and chilli paste. Adjust the quantities according to taste. If tastes vary in your family, make the dishes mild and use a chutney to add heat to the palates of the chilli lovers in your household.

Unusual ingredients

If you're unfamiliar with some ingredients in this book, don't worry – larger supermarkets now stock a wide range of international foods to cater for our diverse population. Or you may find specialist Indian, African or Caribbean grocery shops locally that stock a good variety. We give alternatives for ingredients that may be difficult to source.

Unusual vegetables, fruits and pulses used in this book are ackee, yam, dasheen, okra, bitter melon, green bananas, plantains and pigeon peas. Ackee, a Caribbean and African fruit, is eaten as a vegetable. In the UK it is available canned. Yam, a starchy tuber, can be boiled, roasted, mashed or fried (although it's best to cook it without adding fat) and looks like a pale-fleshed sweet potato. Dasheen (taro) is a starchy tuber that can be roasted, boiled or mashed. Okra, often known as lady fingers due to their long, slim shape, are small green pods with a slightly fuzzy skin and soft white edible seeds. Choose stems that snap cleanly and don't bend. Bitter melon (karela) is an edible vine fruit and

Sample nutritional information

per 100g	LOW fat	LOW saturated fat	MED salt	HIGH sugar
per portion (% of GDA)	395 kcal 20%	13.7g fat 20%	5.2g saturated fat 26%	1.25g salt 21%	3.2g sugars 4%

is one of the most bitter of all fruits. It is similar in size and shape to a cucumber, but with knobbly skin. Green bananas are similar in shape and size to the common banana, but have a firmer texture and are similar in flavour to potato or yam. They don't turn yellow or ripen, unlike the plantain, but are also included in the Eatwell Plate (see page 8) as a starchy food. Pigeon peas (gungo) are usually sold dried but are available canned. They are a source of protein, so make a good meat substitute in soups and stews.

Less unusual ingredients that make an appearance are mung dhal (split mung beans), masoor dhal (split red lentils) and gram flour (chickpea flour or Besan). You may find these in larger supermarkets and in Indian grocers. If you find these items hard to obtain, an online search may help you identify a supplier for them and many of the spices below.

Unusual spices and spice blends that appear in this book include: ajowan seeds (ajwain, carrom or lovage seeds); amchur (a powder made of dried green mangos); cumin-coriander powder (or dhana-jeera, a Gujarati spice blend); panch phoran (a Bengali spice blend; see page 61 for a recipe) and pimento. There are two types of pimento used; ground pimento (allspice) and pimento berries (which look much like peppercorns). Tamarind concentrate, used in the recipe on page 82, is available in Asian, Afro-Caribbean and African grocers and online. Try these also as sources for jaggery, an unrefined cane sugar sold in block form that's used in the recipe on page 93.

Stock

Some recipes call for the use of a stock. Ideally, stock is homemade, as this helps to reduce the salt/sodium content of the dishes you prepare. Try the recipe for vegetable stock here, or look for low-sodium stock cubes or powder and make up as directed on the packaging.

Vegetable stock

1 Put all the ingredients into a large saucepan and cover with about 850ml (1½ pints) water. Bring slowly to the boil, then cover and simmer very gently for 20–30 minutes. Strain and return to the saucepan.

2 Bring back to the boil and bubble vigorously, uncovered, until the liquid has reduced by about a third. Allow to cool. Use this stock within 3 days or freeze.

To freeze: Pour the cooled stock into ice-cube trays and place in the freezer. When frozen, transfer the cubes to a bag, label and return to the freezer.

Makes: about 600ml (20fl oz)
Preparation time: 15 minutes
Cooking time: 1 hour

2 carrots, peeled and thinly sliced

2 onions, roughly chopped

2 sticks celery, roughly chopped

½ bulb fennel, roughly chopped

2 ripe tomatoes, diced

8 chestnut mushrooms, wiped clean and sliced

6 black peppercorns

1 bay leaf

Few sprigs fresh flat-leaf parsley

Snacks, salads

& SIDE DISHES

Dahi vada

This savoury snack of lentil dumplings with a spicy yoghurt topping is a popular Indian street food and makes the perfect hot-weather snack, although it can also be served alongside a main meal. The vadas, or dumplings, are traditionally fried, but this steamed version cuts the fat content significantly and keeps the snack light and healthy without losing any of the flavour.

1 Rinse the dhals and soak them in cold water for 4 hours. Drain the dhals.

2 Place the dhals, the whole green chilli and the water in a food processor and process until you have a thick mixture. Place the mixture in a bowl, cover and leave it in a warm place for 2 hours.

3 To prepare for steaming, place some water in the steamer pan and bring it to the boil. Grease the idli trays or other moulds (see Cook's tip, below) with oil.

4 Add the bicarbonate of soda to the batter and mix thoroughly. Then fill each hollow in the tray, or your improvised moulds, with a tablespoon of batter. Place in the steamer and cook for 10 minutes. Cool the vadas for 5 minutes.

5 When you're ready to serve, whisk together the yoghurt, chilli powder and ground cumin. Spread a few tablespoons of the yoghurt mixture over the base of a shallow serving dish. Arrange the vadas on top and pour the rest of the yoghurt mixture over them. Garnish with roasted ground cumin, chopped coriander and tamarind chutney, if using.

Cook's tip: Idli trays are available from Indian hardware stores and online. They comprise a steamer pan with a stackable set of trays, each with hollows into which you pour the idli batter for steaming. If you don't have access to a set of idli trays, improvise with a conventional steamer and oiled metal dariole moulds, small ramekins or individual silicone muffin cups.

Serves: 8
Preparation time: 15 minutes, plus soaking, fermenting and cooling time
Cooking time: 10 minutes per batch

100g (3½oz) split mung dhal
100g (3½oz) split urad dhal
1 fresh green chilli
2 tablespoons water
Oil for greasing
¼ teaspoon bicarbonate of soda
600ml (1 pint) low-fat natural yoghurt
¼ teaspoon chilli powder
1 teaspoon ground cumin

For the garnish:

1 teaspoon cumin seeds, roasted and ground
3 tablespoons chopped fresh coriander
1 tablespoon tamarind chutney (optional)

per 100 g	LOW	fat	LOW	saturated fat	LOW	salt	MED	sugar
per portion (% of GDA)	239 kcal 12%		2.7g fat 4%		1g saturated fat 5%		0.63g salt 11%	11.8g sugars 13%

Baked vegetable samosas

Serves: 2–3
Preparation time: 30 minutes, plus cooling time
Cooking time: 30–35 minutes

1 baking potato (about 225g/8oz
    unprepared weight), peeled
    and diced

1½ teaspoons olive oil

2 shallots, finely chopped

1 small clove garlic, crushed

1 small fresh chilli, deseeded and
    finely chopped

1 teaspoon ground cumin

1 teaspoon ground coriander

½ teaspoon garam masala, or
    to taste

55g (2oz) frozen peas

55g (2oz) canned chickpeas (drained
    weight), rinsed and drained

2 tablespoons vegetable stock

1 tablespoon tomato purée

1 tablespoon chopped fresh
    coriander

Freshly ground black pepper, to taste

6 sheets filo pastry, defrosted,
    if frozen (each about 30cm x
    18cm/12in x 7in in size)

2 tablespoons sunflower oil, for
    brushing

Mustard seeds, for sprinkling
    (optional)

Traditionally, these pastry parcels filled with deliciously spiced vegetables are deep-fried, making them high in fat. Baking them in the oven greatly reduces the fat content, and using filo pastry for the casing gives these tasty snacks their characteristic crispiness.

1 Put the diced potato in a small pan and cover with water. Bring to the boil, then simmer until tender. Drain well and set aside.

2 Meanwhile, heat the olive oil in a non-stick pan. Add the shallots, garlic and chilli and cook over a medium heat for 5 minutes, stirring occasionally. Now add the ground spices and cook gently for 1 minute, stirring. Add the potatoes and peas and cook for a further minute.

3 Take the pan off the heat and stir in the chickpeas, stock, tomato purée, chopped coriander and black pepper. Lightly crush the potatoes as you stir, if desired. Set the pan aside to allow the mixture to cool.

4 Preheat the oven to 180°C/fan 160°C/gas mark 4. Cut each sheet of filo pastry in half lengthwise to make 12 30cm x 9cm (12in x 3½in) strips. Place 1 strip on a work surface, with a short edge nearest to you. Brush the strip with sunflower oil, place a spoonful of the cooled filling on the bottom right corner of the pastry strip, then fold the pastry over the filling into a triangle shape. Fold the pastry upwards and away from you 4 more times, maintaining the triangular shape. Tuck in the remaining narrow strip of pastry into the last fold at the end to create a triangular samosa. Brush the samosa all over with a little sunflower oil. Now repeat with the remaining filo strips and filling to make 12 samosas.

5 Place the samosas on a non-stick baking sheet, sprinkle with mustard seeds, if using, and bake for 20–25 minutes or until crisp and deep golden-brown in colour. Serve immediately, or cool slightly before serving.

per 100g	MED fat	LOW saturated fat	LOW salt	LOW sugar
per portion (% of GDA)	323 kcal 16%	15g fat 21%	1.7g saturated fat 9%	0.3g salt 5%	4g sugars 4%

Hara bhara kebabs

Serves: 6
Preparation time: 30 minutes
Cooking time: 8 minutes

100g (3½oz) white or red potatoes, peeled and boiled

100g (3½oz) peas, cooked

100g (3½oz) fresh spinach, finely chopped

2 fresh green chillies, finely chopped

1 teaspoon finely grated fresh root ginger

2 tablespoons roughly chopped fresh coriander

3 tablespoons cornflour

3 teaspoons olive oil

These tasty patties are light, healthy and easy to make. 'Hara bhara' means 'filled with greens' in Hindi and, unlike the typical Indian kebab, which is made with meat, these are full of healthy green veg – spinach, peas and coriander. Try them with raitha and a crispy salad.

1 In a large bowl, mix together all the ingredients except the oil. Mash the mixture until it is fairly smooth.

2 Take a spoonful of the mixture and roll it into a ball that's roughly the size of a golf ball. Now flatten the ball into a patty. Repeat with the remaining mixture.

3 Heat the oil in a heavy-based frying pan and lightly fry the patties for 2 minutes on each side. Drain on kitchen paper. Serve hot.

Cook's tip: You can prepare the patties, up to the end of step 2, a day in advance and store them in the refrigerator. Fry them when you are ready to serve.

per 100g	LOW fat	LOW saturated fat	LOW salt	LOW sugar
per portion (% of GDA)	**73 kcal** 4%	**2g fat** 3%	**0.5g saturated fat** 3%	**0.1g salt** 2%	**1g sugars** 1%

Dhokri

Serves: 6
Preparation time: 5–10 minutes, plus fermenting time
Cooking time: 10–15 minutes

50ml (2fl oz) warm water

100ml (3½fl oz) low-fat natural yoghurt

175g (6oz) gram flour

¼ teaspoon turmeric

¼ teaspoon ground coriander

½ teaspoon coarsely ground black pepper

¼ teaspoon roasted cumin seeds

½ teaspoon crushed fresh green chillies

¼ teaspoon asafoetida

¼ teaspoon sesame seeds

¼ teaspoon ground ajowan seeds

1 tablespoon finely chopped fresh coriander

1 teaspoon rapeseed oil, plus extra for greasing

¾ teaspoon bicarbonate of soda

This mouthwatering savoury cake is a classic Gujarati snack (Gujarat, in Northwest India, has an interesting cuisine that is famous throughout the world). Its wonderful sponge-like texture makes this dish very light, and it is healthier than the average Indian snack as it is steamed, not fried. Serve dhokri with red or green chutney (see page 106).

1 Mix the warm water with the yoghurt in a bowl, then add the gram flour to form a thick, smooth paste.

2 Mix in the turmeric, ground coriander and black pepper, then cover and leave the paste in a warm place for 10 hours.

3 Boil some water in a pan that's large enough to hold a 25cm (10in) steel or aluminium dish. You will steam the batter in this dish, which will be placed inside the pan. To ensure the boiling water doesn't get into the dish during steaming, place a trivet in the pan for the dish to sit on. Grease the dish lightly with oil, place it in the pan, ready for steaming, and cover with the pan lid.

4 While the water is coming to the boil, add to the dhokri paste the cumin seeds, crushed chillies, asafoetida, sesame seeds, ground ajowan seeds, coriander and oil and mix thoroughly. When the water is boiling and you're ready to steam the batter, add the bicarbonate of soda and mix well. Now pour the mixture into the dish, replace the lid and steam for 10–15 minutes.

5 Tentatively touch the dhokri with the flat of your hand. If it doesn't stick to your hand, it is cooked. Remove the dhokri dish from the steamer, allow the dhokri to cool, then cut it into cubes.

Cook's tip: Self-raising flour or raising agents such as bicarbonate of soda contain sodium, so using them will affect the salt content of your dish.

per 100g	MED fat		LOW saturated fat		MED salt		LOW sugar	
per portion (% of GDA)	107 kcal	5%	2.4g fat	3%	0.1g saturated fat	1%	0.8g salt	13%	1.4g sugars	2%

Chicken & egg wrap

The ingenious use of parathas (Indian flatbreads) for wrapping, coupled with the spicy filling, gives these wraps a lovely Indian twist. They are great when hot from the pan, wrapped up and served immediately, but work equally well when cold, making them perfect picnic fare. Serve these wraps alone or with some green chutney (see page 106) mixed with yoghurt.

1 First, marinate the chicken for the filling. Mix together all the filling ingredients except for the oil. Cover and marinate in the refrigerator for 2 hours.

2 To make the parathas, sift the flour into a large bowl. Add the oil, milk and 1 egg and knead for 7–10 minutes. Place the dough in a bowl, cover with a damp cloth and leave in a warm place for 20 minutes.

3 Divide the dough into 6 balls. On a floured surface, roll out each ball into a circle that is 16–17cm (6¼–6½in) across and 5mm (¼in) thick.

4 Beat the remaining 3 eggs in a bowl. Heat a frying pan and put a paratha into the hot pan. After 1 minute, turn it over. Put 1–2 tablespoons of beaten egg on the paratha and spread it out. Immediately turn over the paratha again and cook the egged side for 30 seconds. Transfer the paratha to a plate and repeat with the remaining paratha-dough rounds. Set aside.

5 Half an hour before you start cooking the chicken, put 6 wooden skewers into cold water to soak until cooking time. Preheat the grill on a medium setting, or the oven to 180°C/fan 160°C/gas mark 4, or prepare the barbecue for cooking. Skewer the chicken and grill, bake or barbecue it for 20 minutes, until the chicken is cooked through. Baste with the oil half way through cooking.

6 To make the wraps, put some cooked chicken in the centre of each paratha and roll them up. Serve with the onion slices.

Serves: 6
Preparation time: 30 minutes, plus marinating and proving time
Cooking time: 30 minutes

For the filling:

2 skinless, boneless chicken breasts, cut into 2.5cm (1in) cubes

1 clove garlic, crushed

1 teaspoon grated fresh root ginger

1 teaspoon ground cumin

¼ teaspoon turmeric

Pinch of garam masala

2 fresh green chillies, finely chopped

1 teaspoon tomato purée

1 teaspoon lemon juice

1 tablespoon rapeseed oil

For the parathas:

200g (7oz) plain flour, plus extra for dusting

1 teaspoon rapeseed oil

100ml (3½fl oz) semi-skimmed milk

4 small eggs

To serve:

2 red onions, thinly sliced

per 100g	MED fat		LOW saturated fat		LOW salt		LOW sugar	
per portion (% of GDA)	248 kcal	12%	7.5g fat	11%	1.7g saturated fat	9%	0.21g salt	4%	1.3g sugars	1%

Thai sweet chilli chicken wraps

Serves: 2
Preparation time: 10 minutes
Cooking time: none

**2 plain wheat-flour tortilla (deli)
wraps (each about 25cm/10in
in diameter)**

**2 tablespoons Thai sweet chilli sauce
or sweet chilli sauce, plus extra for
dipping (optional)**

**150g (5½oz) cooked skinless,
boneless chicken breast,
thinly sliced**

35g (1¼oz) baby spinach leaves

4 spring onions, chopped

**1 vine-ripened tomato, thinly sliced
(optional)**

Freshly ground black pepper, to taste

**Few sprigs or 2 teaspoons chopped
fresh coriander (optional)**

**When you're in need of a substantial savoury snack or a good
lunchbox idea, these wraps are ideal. Sweet chilli sauce is the
perfect complement to chicken, and the spinach, tomato and
coriander make the wraps wonderfully fresh.**

1 Spread one side of each tortilla wrap with a little chilli sauce. Arrange some
chicken slices and spinach leaves across the middle of each wrap. Scatter
over the spring onions and top with tomato slices (if using). Season the
filling with black pepper, then sprinkle with chopped coriander or lay over
the coriander sprigs (if using).

2 Fold or loosely roll up the tortillas to enclose the filling. Cut each into 3 or
4 sections to serve. Serve immediately.

Variations: Try using wholemeal or flavoured tortilla wraps instead of
plain white ones. Mango chutney, chunky tomato salsa or reduced-calorie
mayonnaise can be substituted for the chilli sauce. Serve with extra chilli sauce
for dipping, if desired. Try spreading the wraps with a little low-fat soft cheese
before adding the sweet chilli sauce. Warm the wraps according to the packet
instructions before adding the filling, if preferred.

per 100g	LOW fat		LOW saturated fat		MED salt		MED sugar	
per portion (% of GDA)	235 kcal 12%	0.9g fat 1%	0.1g saturated fat 1%		0.9g salt 15%		11.7g sugars 13%	

Spicy dasheen

Serves: 6
Preparation time: 15 minutes
Cooking time: 30 minutes

500g (1lb 2oz) dasheen, peeled and cut into bite-sized cubes

1 tablespoon mustard oil

1 teaspoon turmeric

2 teaspoons mild curry powder

1 teaspoon oregano seeds

Scotch bonnet pepper, to taste, finely sliced

4 fresh curry leaves

Lemon juice, to taste

Dasheen, also known as taro, is thought to be one of the earliest cultivated plants and is grown for its leaves and roots. This side dish of spicy dasheen makes a great accompaniment to grilled fish and vegetables, or use a chapati (see page 99) as a wrap to turn it into a substantial main meal in itself. Look for dasheen in West Indian supermarkets, or in large supermarkets where there is a sizeable West Indian community in the neighbourhood.

1 Cook the dasheen in boiling water until tender – you should be able to pierce the flesh easily with a fork. Drain and set aside.

2 Heat the mustard oil in a non-stick pan and add the turmeric, curry powder, oregano seeds, Scotch bonnet pepper and curry leaves. Fry gently for 1–2 minutes.

3 Increase the heat to high and stir in the dasheen. Finish with a squeeze of lemon juice. Serve hot.

Variation: Substitute potato for the dasheen.

per 100g	LOW fat	LOW saturated fat	LOW salt	LOW sugar
per portion (% of GDA)	**100 kcal** 5%	**2.1g fat** 3% **0.2g saturated fat** 1%	**0g salt** 0%	**0.9g sugars** 1%

Baigan choka

This Caribbean dish of roasted aubergines is very tasty, largely because cooking aubergines directly over the flame in this way gives them a deliciously smoky flavour that's very savoury and satisfying. It also gives them a lovely melt-in-your-mouth texture. A great accompaniment to curried meat or fish, this dish also makes a good meal in itself when served up in a wrap.

1 Wash the aubergines and make slits in them with a knife, then stuff the slits with garlic. Roast the aubergines on a roasting rack set on the hob directly over a medium flame, or under a medium grill, until soft.

2 Slice the aubergines in half, scrape out the pulp and discard the skin. Put the pulp in a large bowl, add the remaining ingredients and mash them together using a fork.

3 Gently cook the aubergine mixture in a non-stick frying pan for 5–7 minutes. Serve hot.

Serves: 4
Preparation time: 10 minutes
Cooking time: 20 minutes

2 large aubergines
2 cloves garlic, finely chopped
½ medium onion, chopped
2 medium tomatoes, chopped
Freshly ground black pepper, to taste
Small bunch fresh coriander, finely chopped
1 teaspoon curry powder

per 100g	LOW fat	LOW saturated fat	LOW salt	LOW sugar
per portion (% of GDA)	**40 kcal** 2%	**0.7g fat** 1%	**0.6g saturated fat** 3%	**0g salt** 0%	**4.5g sugars** 5%

Spiced roast roots

Serves: 2–3
Preparation time: 20 minutes
Cooking time: 30–40 minutes

700g (1lb 9oz) mixed root vegetables, such as sweet potatoes, parsnips, carrots and swede

4 teaspoons olive oil

1–2 teaspoons hot chilli powder

1–2 teaspoons ground cumin

1–2 teaspoons ground coriander

1 clove garlic, finely chopped (optional)

1 tablespoon sunflower or pumpkin seeds

Freshly ground black pepper, to taste

2–3 teaspoons chopped fresh coriander (optional)

The combination of sweetness and spiciness works well in this tasty side dish. Spiced roast roots are great served alongside Indian food or a roast dinner, and with grilled or barbecued meat. Alternatively, throw them into a big bowl of salad leaves for an interesting and substantial salad.

1 Preheat the oven to 200°C/fan 180°C/gas mark 6. Peel the root vegetables, cut them into 2.5cm (1in) pieces and set aside. Whisk together the olive oil and ground spices in a small dish.

2 Tip the diced vegetables into a non-stick roasting tin, then scatter over the garlic (if using). Drizzle the oil mixture over the vegetables and toss them in the oil to coat them. Shake the tin to redistribute the vegetables into a single layer.

3 Roast the vegetables, turning them once or twice, for 30–40 minutes or until they are tinged brown. During the last 5–10 minutes of the cooking time, sprinkle over the seeds and return the roasting tin to the oven for the remainder of the cooking time. Remove from the oven, season with black pepper and sprinkle with chopped coriander, if desired. Serve hot.

Cook's tip: Grind whole spices, such as cumin and coriander seeds, just before use to get the best flavour.

per 100g	MED fat		LOW saturated fat		LOW salt		MED sugar	
per portion (% of GDA)	138 kcal	7%	5g fat	7%	1g saturated fat	5%	0.1g salt	2%	11g sugars	12%

Spicy plantains & spinach

Serves: 4
Preparation time: 10 minutes
Cooking time: 40 minutes

2 firm, ripe plantains that are yellow
in colour

1 tablespoon rapeseed oil

2 spring onions, finely chopped

1 red pepper, deseeded and thinly
sliced

1 tablespoon finely chopped fresh
root ginger

½ teaspoon mild curry powder

Scotch bonnet pepper, to taste,
chopped

2 fresh tomatoes, chopped

Freshly ground black pepper, to taste

200g (7oz) fresh spinach, finely
chopped

This delicious West Indian dish is perfect served alongside meat or fish and a portion of vegetables. Plantains are a Caribbean staple, often used to provide the starchy carbohydrate element in a meal, which can make a wonderful change from rice- or wheat-based carbohydrates.

1 Make an incision along the length of each plantain so that it's easier to peel once cooked. Boil in water for 10–15 minutes or until the plantain can be easily pierced with a fork. Drain and leave to cool.

2 Heat the rapeseed oil in a large non-stick pan. Add the spring onion, red pepper and ginger and fry for 5 minutes. Then add the curry powder, Scotch bonnet pepper and tomato and cook gently for 2–5 minutes until the vegetables have softened. Season with black pepper to taste. Meanwhile, peel the plantains, discard the skin and slice into discs about 2.5cm (1in) thick.

3 Transfer the plantains to the pan, add the spinach and mix well. Cook for 2–3 minutes until the plantains are flavoured with the spicy mixture and the spinach leaves have just wilted.

per 100g	LOW fat		LOW saturated fat		LOW salt		LOW sugar	
per portion (% of GDA)	180 kcal	9%	3.5g fat	5%	0.6g saturated fat 3%	0.2g salt	3%	10.8g sugars 12%

Low-fat spicy chips

Serves: 4
Preparation time: 5 minutes
Cooking time: 20 minutes

450g (1lb) potatoes, peeled
1 tablespoon olive oil
1 teaspoon lemon juice
½ teaspoon chilli powder

Oven-baked potatoes infused with Indian spices – what could be more comforting? These delicious spicy chips are much healthier than their fried counterparts, but just as flavoursome. Serve them alongside any Indian meal or with grilled meat or fish.

1 Preheat the oven to 180°C/fan 160°C/gas mark 4.

2 Slice the peeled potatoes into 2cm (¾in) thick rounds. Blanch them in boiling water for 2 minutes, then drain the potatoes and return them to the pan.

3 Mix the oil, lemon juice and chilli powder in a small jug. Pour this mixture over the chips and toss them in the pan to coat them evenly in the lemon-juice-and-oil mixture.

4 Place the chips on a non-stick cooking mat set in a baking tray. Bake the chips for 15–20 minutes, turning them as necessary, until they are cooked through and golden brown. Serve immediately.

per 100g	LOW fat		LOW saturated fat		LOW salt		LOW sugar	
per portion (% of GDA)	**116 kcal** 6%	**4g fat** 6%	**0.5g saturated fat** 3%	**0.0g salt** 0%	**1g sugars** 1%

Pigeon pea salad

In the Caribbean, pigeon peas are also known as gungo, gunga or congo peas, and are particularly popular in Jamaica, where they are a favourite choice for Sunday rice and peas. This dish makes a great lunchtime salad.

1 Rinse the pigeon peas in cold water and drain well. Put them in a large bowl with the sweetcorn and grated carrot.

2 Combine all the ingredients for the dressing in a large bowl and season with black pepper to taste. Pour the dressing over the peas, sweetcorn and grated carrot, mixing well. Add the chopped spring onions to garnish. Serve immediately.

Cook's tip: If using dried pigeon peas, soak them overnight in cold water, then drain. Boil them rapidly in fresh water for at least 10 minutes, then simmer for 30–50 minutes until tender. There is no need to add salt. Drain the peas and leave to cool, then use them in place of the canned pigeon peas in this recipe.

Serves: 4
Preparation time: 15 minutes
Cooking time: none

400g (14oz) can green pigeon peas
200g (7oz) can sweetcorn in unsalted water, drained
2 medium carrots, peeled and grated
2 spring onions, finely chopped

For the dressing:
3 tablespoons olive oil
1 tablespoon honey
1 tablespoon balsamic vinegar
Juice of 1 lime
1 small Scotch bonnet pepper, deseeded and finely chopped
1 teaspoon finely chopped garlic
Handful of fresh parsley, roughly chopped
Freshly ground black pepper, to taste

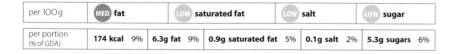

per 100g	MED fat	LOW saturated fat	LOW salt	LOW sugar
per portion (% of GDA)	174 kcal 9%	6.3g fat 9%	0.9g saturated fat 5%	0.1g salt 2%	5.3g sugars 6%

Tomato & onion salad

Serves: 4
Preparation time: 5 minutes
Cooking time: none

2 large, firm, ripe tomatoes
1 medium onion
½ teaspoon finely chopped
 fresh coriander
½ teaspoon chilli powder
1 teaspoon lemon juice

This simple side salad is the perfect dish to serve with Indian food and can be whipped together very quickly. Serve it alongside meat or vegetable rice such as Vegetable Biriyani (see page 90) or kebabs such as Mutton Kebabs (see page 49).

1 Chop the tomatoes into 2.5cm (1in) pieces and the onion into 1cm (½in) pieces, and place them in a large bowl.

2 Mix the coriander with the tomatoes and onions.

3 Just before serving, sprinkle over the chilli powder and lemon juice.

per 100g	LOW fat	LOW saturated fat	LOW salt	LOW sugar
per portion (% of GDA)	**32 kcal** 2%	**0.8g fat** 1%	**0.0g saturated fat** 0%	**0.1g salt** 2%	**4.5g sugars** 5%

Jewelled couscous salad

Serves: 6
Preparation time: 30 minutes
Cooking time: none

300g (10½oz) wholewheat couscous

400ml (14fl oz) hot vegetable stock (preferably homemade – see page 13)

400g (14oz) can chickpeas, rinsed and drained

1 red pepper, deseeded and diced

1 bunch spring onions, chopped

1 small fresh red chilli, deseeded and finely chopped, or to taste

85g (3oz) ready-to-eat dried apricots, chopped

4 medjool dates, stoned and chopped

Seeds from ½–1 pomegranate (optional)

For the dressing:

4 tablespoons olive oil

1 tablespoon freshly squeezed orange juice

1 teaspoon finely grated orange zest

2 teaspoons white wine vinegar

2 teaspoons clear (runny) honey

2 tablespoons finely chopped fresh coriander

Freshly ground black pepper, to taste

Substantial and colourful, this salad is equally delicious served warm or chilled. This versatility, coupled with the fact that it's such a pretty dish, makes it ideal for entertaining.

1 Put the couscous in a heatproof bowl, pour over the hot stock and stir. Cover with clingfilm or a tea towel and set aside for the amount of time indicated on the packet instructions (about 6 minutes), until the stock has been absorbed.

2 Meanwhile, combine the chickpeas, red pepper, spring onions, chilli, apricots and dates in a large serving bowl and set aside.

3 To make the dressing, put the olive oil, orange juice, orange zest, vinegar, honey, coriander and black pepper in a small bowl and whisk together until thoroughly combined.

4 Fluff up the couscous with a fork, then add it to the chickpea mixture together with dressing. Stir well to mix. Serve the salad warm or cooled, or chill before serving. Just before serving, sprinkle the pomegranate seeds (if using) over the salad.

Variations: Add 175–225g (6–8oz) cooked skinless, boneless chicken, diced, to the salad with the chickpeas, if you like. Omit the pomegranate seeds and sprinkle over 2–4 tablespoons of toasted sesame seeds, sunflower seeds or pumpkin seeds instead.

per 100g	**MED** fat		**LOW** saturated fat		**LOW** salt		**MED** sugar	
per portion (% of GDA)	329 kcal	16%	8.5g fat 12%	1.1g saturated fat 6%	0g salt 0%		20.5g sugars 23%	

Avocado & papaya salad

Serves: 4
Preparation time: 10 minutes
Cooking time: none

4 ripe avocados, peeled and stoned

4 ripe papayas, peeled and deseeded

Juice of 1 lime

2 baby gem lettuces, washed and trimmed

2 handfuls of cherry tomatoes, halved

1 small red onion, finely diced

For the dressing:

1 clove garlic, finely chopped

Zest of 2 limes and juice of 1

¼ teaspoon sugar

½ teaspoon freshly ground black pepper

½ teaspoon cayenne pepper

60ml (2¼fl oz) olive oil

These two fruits make a pleasing combination, especially with the hint of spiciness from the cayenne pepper and the freshness of the lime juice – a taste of the tropics in a bowl!

1 Slice the avocados lengthwise into 1cm (½in) slices. Slice the papayas widthwise into 1cm (½in) slices. Drizzle with the juice of 1 lime immediately.

2 Create a bed of baby gem lettuce in each of 4 bowls. On top of this, arrange the avocado and papaya slices, overlapping and alternating them. Now add the cherry tomatoes and onions to each bowl.

3 Combine the dressing ingredients in a small jug or bowl, mix well and pour or spoon over the salad. Serve immediately.

Variation: Use mangoes in place of the papayas.

per 100g	MED fat		LOW saturated fat		LOW salt		LOW sugar	
per portion (% of GDA)	440 kcal	22%	33.6g fat	48%	6.6g saturated fat	33%	0.2g salt	3%	7.2g sugars	8%

Meat

DISHES

Chicken pilau rice

Fragrant rice combines well with chicken in this delicious dish. Serve the pilau with a crunchy salad made of cucumbers, finely sliced onion and tomatoes, or with cucumber raitha.

Serves: 10
Preparation time: 10 minutes, plus soaking time
Cooking time: 30–40 minutes

225g (8oz) Basmati rice

400g (14oz) chicken

1 tablespoon rapeseed oil

1 medium onion, chopped

1 teaspoon crushed fresh root ginger

1½ teaspoons crushed garlic

1 large tomato, chopped

1 teaspoon ground cinnamon

½ teaspoon ground cloves

1 teaspoon crushed fresh green chillies

1 teaspoon garam masala

600ml (1 pint) water

1 Rinse the rice and leave it to soak in cold water for 20 minutes.

2 Remove the skin from the chicken and discard it, then cut the chicken into bite-sized pieces. Transfer the chicken pieces to a pan and add just enough cold water to cover the meat. Bring to the boil. As soon as the water starts to boil, turn off the heat and drain off the water.

3 Heat the oil in a large non-stick pan. Add the onion and cook until brown. Stir in the ginger and garlic, then the tomato. Cook for a minute, then add the cinnamon, cloves, green chillies and garam masala, followed by the chicken pieces.

4 Add 50ml (2fl oz) of the water and cook over a high heat for 5 minutes. Then reduce the heat and simmer for 10 minutes.

6 Now add the rice and the remaining water. Cover and cook over a high heat until the liquid starts to boil, then reduce the heat to low and cook until all the water has evaporated. Remove from the heat and allow to stand for 5–10 minutes before serving.

Variation: You can substitute mutton for the chicken. Ensure you trim any fat off the meat first.

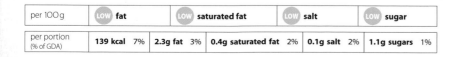

per 100g	LOW fat	LOW saturated fat	LOW salt	LOW sugar
per portion (% of GDA)	**139 kcal** 7%	**2.3g fat** 3%	**0.4g saturated fat** 2%	**0.1g salt** 2%	**1.1g sugars** 1%

Oven-baked chicken

Serves: 4
Preparation time: 15 minutes, plus marinating time
Cooking time: 45–55 minutes

675g (1lb 8oz) whole chicken
50ml (2fl oz) low-fat natural yoghurt
1 tablespoon soy sauce
1½ teaspoons crushed garlic
2½ teaspoons crushed fresh root ginger
2 teaspoons lemon juice
2 tablespoons chopped fresh coriander
2 tablespoons chopped fresh fenugreek leaves
1 teaspoon coarsely ground black pepper
1 teaspoon garam masala
1 teaspoon ground cinnamon
½ teaspoon ground cloves
Cooking spray or oil, for greasing
3 large tomatoes, sliced
1 green pepper, deseeded and sliced
2 large onions, sliced

Chicken is delicious when it has been marinated in a spicy sauce, as here. Served with a helping of lightly steamed vegetables, this dish makes a very satisfying and healthy evening meal. The marinade used in this recipe is great with barbecued chicken, too.

1 Remove the skin and all visible fat from the chicken and joint the bird into quarters. Using a sharp knife, make deep slits in the flesh. Put the chicken in a bowl, cover and refrigerate.

2 Mix together the yoghurt, soy sauce, garlic, ginger, lemon juice, coriander, fenugreek and all the spices – you can blend them in a liquidizer, if you like. Pour this mixture over the chicken, ensuring you cover all the flesh and fill the slits you made in the flesh. Leave the chicken to marinate in the refrigerator for 4 hours.

3 Preheat the oven to 180°C/fan 160°C/gas mark 4. Spray a non-stick frying pan with oil and cook the marinated chicken over a high heat until lightly browned.

4 Remove the chicken from the pan and place it in an ovenproof dish. Arrange the slices of tomatoes, pepper and onions on top and cover the dish with foil.

5 Bake the chicken and vegetables in the preheated oven for 30 minutes, then reduce the heat to 140°C/fan 120°C/gas mark 1 and cook for a further 15–20 minutes or until cooked through. To check if it is done, pierce through the thickest part of a leg joint and breast joint with a metal skewer – if the juices run clear, the meat is cooked. Serve with the tomatoes, pepper and onions alongside the chicken.

Variation: To barbecue the chicken, carry out steps 1, 2 and 3, above. After browning, cook the chicken pieces over medium-hot coals for 25–30 minutes, basting with any left-over marinade.

per 100g	LOW fat		LOW saturated fat		LOW salt		LOW sugar	
per portion (% of GDA)	**187 kcal** 9%	**3g fat** 4%	**1g saturated fat** 5%		**0.9g salt** 15%		**13g sugars** 14%	

Black pepper chicken

Serves: 6
Preparation time: 5 minutes, plus marinating time
Cooking time: 25–30 minutes

3 teaspoons rapeseed oil

1 teaspoon finely grated fresh root ginger

2 cloves garlic, crushed

1 teaspoon coarsely ground black pepper

1 teaspoon ground white pepper

1 medium onion, finely chopped

6 skinless, boneless chicken breasts (about 900g/2lb unprepared weight), cut into bite-sized pieces

2 fresh green chillies, slit lengthwise

200ml (7fl oz) boiling water

2 teaspoons lemon juice

2 tablespoons finely chopped fresh coriander

Served with Basmati rice and a yoghurt salad, this easy one-pot meal makes the perfect after-work supper or weekend lunch. Even the marinating time is quick, but you could, of course, extend that to allow the flavours of the spices to infuse the meat further.

1 Mix 1 teaspoon of the oil with the ginger, garlic and the black and white pepper and rub this mixture into the chicken pieces. Cover and marinate in the refrigerator for at least 30 minutes.

2 Heat the remaining oil in a wok and fry the onion for 2 minutes or until it is translucent.

3 Add the marinated chicken pieces to the wok and gently stir-fry for about 10 minutes, until the chicken is golden brown.

4 Add the chillies and water, cover and simmer for 10 minutes or until the chicken is cooked. To make a thicker or more concentrated sauce, remove the lid to allow some of the water to evaporate and continue cooking for another 5 minutes.

5 Take the wok off the heat, then stir in the lemon juice and sprinkle the coriander leaves on top before serving.

Cook's tip: If you prefer a drier curry, marinate the chicken as described in step 1. Preheat the oven to 180°C/fan 160°C/gas mark 4. Place the marinated chicken on a baking tray and bake for about 15 minutes until the chicken is cooked through.

To freeze: Allow the dish to cool completely, then transfer to a rigid freezer-proof container. Cover, seal and label, and freeze for up to 1 month. To serve, defrost completely, then reheat thoroughly.

per 100g	LOW fat	LOW saturated fat	LOW salt	LOW sugar
per portion (% of GDA)	**189 kcal** 9%	**3.3g fat** 5% / **0.6g saturated fat** 3%	**0.3g salt** 5%	**1.4g sugars** 2%

Chicken tikka masala

You can serve chicken tikka masala with plain Basmati rice or in a pitta pocket with lettuce and sliced onions.

1 Blend together the yoghurt, garlic, ginger, black pepper and chilli paste in a bowl until well mixed, then spoon this mixture over the chicken. Allow the chicken to marinate in the refrigerator for 1–2 hours.

2 Heat the oil in a large pan, add the cumin seeds and chopped onion and cook over a medium heat until brown.

3 Remove the chicken pieces from the marinade and add them to the pan. Cook over a high heat for about 5 minutes.

4 Stir in the fenugreek, tomato purée, garam masala and ground cumin-coriander powder. Then reduce the heat and simmer for 15–20 minutes or until the chicken is cooked and the liquid has evaporated.

5 Stir in the crème fraîche. Adjust the consistency of the sauce with a little water, if liked, and heat through, then stir in the coriander before serving.

Serves: 6
Preparation time: 10 minutes, plus marinating time
Cooking time: 25–30 minutes

3 tablespoons low-fat natural yoghurt

2 teaspoons crushed garlic

2 teaspoons crushed fresh root ginger

1 teaspoon coarsely ground black pepper

1 teaspoon red chilli paste or crushed fresh red chillies

450g (1lb) skinless chicken breasts, cut into bite-sized pieces

1 tablespoon rapeseed oil

1 teaspoon cumin seeds

1 medium onion, chopped

1 tablespoon chopped fresh fenugreek leaves

2 tablespoons tomato purée

1 teaspoon garam masala

1½ teaspoons cumin-coriander powder

2 tablespoons half-fat crème fraîche

1 tablespoon chopped fresh coriander

per 100g	MED fat		LOW saturated fat		LOW salt		LOW sugar	
per portion (% of GDA)	136 kcal	7%	4.9g fat 7%	1.3g saturated fat 7%	0.2g salt	3%	2.4g sugars	3%

Chicken Jalfrezi

Serves: 2
Preparation time: 10 minutes
Cooking time: 15–18 minutes

2 teaspoons olive oil

1 onion, chopped

1 clove garlic, chopped

1 fresh green chilli, deseeded and
   chopped

2 teaspoons curry powder or paste

1 teaspoon tomato purée

2 skinless chicken breasts, cut into
   bite-sized pieces

125ml (4fl oz) water

1 teaspoon grated fresh root ginger

1 green pepper, deseeded and sliced

This tasty chicken curry is a relatively dry curry as it has less 'masala' (spicy gravy), so it is great served with chapatis (see page 99) or any Indian flatbread of your choice. Try serving this curry with Tomato and Onion Salad (see page 32) as a side dish.

1 Heat the oil in a large pan, then add the onion, garlic and chilli and fry for about 4 minutes.

2 Stir in the curry powder or paste and the tomato purée. Stir for 30 seconds, then add the chicken.

3 Brown the meat quickly over a high heat for 3–4 minutes, then add the water and cook for 6–8 minutes. Stir, add the ginger and green pepper and cook for 1 minute.

Variation: Use cubed lean pork in place of the chicken.

Cook's tip: If you don't have any curry powder or paste, add ¼ teaspoon turmeric, ½ teaspoon ground cumin, and ½ teaspoon ground coriander to the dish just before adding the tomato purée. If you don't have tomato purée, use 1 chopped fresh tomato instead.

To freeze: Allow the dish to cool completely, then transfer to a rigid freezer-proof container. Cover, seal and label, and freeze for up to 1 month. To serve, defrost completely, then reheat thoroughly.

per 100g	LOW fat	LOW saturated fat	LOW salt	LOW sugar
per portion (% of GDA)	**227 kcal** 11%	**5.5g fat** 8%	**1g saturated fat** 5%	**0.3g salt** 5%	**5.8g sugars** 6%

Chicken & green beans korma

Serves: 2
Preparation time: 10 minutes
Cooking time: 45 minutes

2 teaspoons sunflower oil

1 small onion, finely chopped

1cm (½in) piece of fresh root ginger, peeled and finely chopped

1 clove garlic, crushed

4–5 teaspoons medium curry powder or curry paste

4 skinless, boneless chicken thigh fillets (about 300g/10½oz total unprepared weight), cut into bite-sized pieces

100ml (3½fl oz) chicken stock

4 tablespoons reduced-fat crème fraîche

1 teaspoon tomato purée

Freshly ground black pepper, to taste

100g (3½oz) green beans, trimmed and halved or cut into 4cm (1½in) lengths

20g (¾oz) ground almonds

Chopped fresh coriander, to garnish (optional)

Korma recipes are usually quite high in fat, but this dish is healthier than the average chicken korma because it uses skinless chicken and reduced-fat crème fraîche. With the addition of lots of fresh green beans, this curry is a healthier alternative to a take-away. Serve with plain Basmati rice.

1 Heat the sunflower oil in a non-stick pan. Add the onion, ginger and garlic and cook gently for about 5 minutes or until the onion begins to soften, stirring occasionally. Stir in the curry powder and cook for 1 minute, stirring. Add the chicken and cook over a medium heat for about 5 minutes or until the chicken is lightly coloured all over, stirring occasionally.

2 Stir in the stock, crème fraîche, tomato purée and black pepper. Bring to the boil, stirring continuously, then reduce the heat, cover and simmer for 15 minutes, stirring occasionally. Stir in the green beans, then cover and cook for a further 10–15 minutes or until the chicken is cooked through and beans are tender, stirring occasionally.

3 Stir in the ground almonds and simmer, uncovered, for 1–2 minutes or until the sauce has thickened. Remove from the heat and garnish with the chopped coriander (if using).

Cook's tip: For a stronger curry flavour, use a hot curry powder or curry paste of your choice and add to taste.

Variations: Substitute skinless, boneless chicken breast fillets or turkey thigh meat for the chicken thigh fillets. Use fresh or frozen peas or broad beans instead of the green beans, if you like.

per 100g	MED fat	MED saturated fat	LOW salt	LOW sugar
per portion (% of GDA)	**392 kcal** 20%	**21g fat** 30%	**6g saturated fat** 30%	**0.7g salt** 12%	**6.7g sugars** 7%

Brown stew chicken

Serves: 8
Preparation time: 15 minutes, plus marinating time
Cooking time: 1 hour

1 clove garlic, crushed

1 tablespoon soy sauce

1 medium onion, chopped

1 teaspoon coarsely ground black pepper

Juice of 1 lime

Scotch bonnet pepper, to taste, sliced

6 chicken thigh and leg joints, skin removed

1 carrot, peeled and diced

1 green or red pepper, deseeded and sliced

2 large tomatoes, chopped

1 tablespoon tomato purée

250ml (9fl oz) water

3 sprigs fresh thyme

This satisfying West Indian dish is a great winter warmer. Traditionally, the marinade contains sugar, but the sweet/savoury flavour of the soy sauce and the fieriness of the Scotch bonnet chilli make this dish delicious without it. Serve hot, with some Rice and Peas (see page 92) or plain boiled rice.

1 Mix the garlic, soy sauce, half the chopped onion, the black pepper, lime juice and Scotch bonnet pepper together in a small bowl or jug. Place the chicken in an ovenproof dish and coat it with the marinade. Marinate in the refrigerator for about 2 hours or overnight, if possible.

2 Preheat the oven to 190°C/fan 170°C/gas mark 5. Put the remaining ingredients into the ovenproof dish, mix with the chicken and the marinade, cover the dish with a tight-fitting lid and cook, turning frequently, for 40–60 minutes or until the juices run clear when the flesh is pierced with a small knife through the thickest part.

per 100g	LOW fat	LOW saturated fat	LOW salt	LOW sugar
per portion (% of GDA)	**180 kcal** 9%	**7.7g fat** 11%	**2.2g saturated fat** 11%	**0.5g salt** 8%	**4.5g sugars** 5%

Mutton kebabs

Mutton kebabs tend to be quite high in fat, but using lean mince makes all the difference. Serve these kebabs in pitta pockets with crispy salad leaves. They're ideal to take on a picnic, too, as they are great hot or cold.

1 Mix together the minced meat, chillies, garam masala, chilli powder, garlic and ginger in a large bowl. Cover and marinate in the refrigerator for 2 hours.

2 Preheat the grill on a medium setting. Add the onion and coriander to the meat mixture and mix well.

3 Flour your hands using the plain flour or gram flour, then mould the mixture into 20 sausage shapes.

4 Place the kebabs on a wire rack in a grill pan – this will allow the fat to drain off the meat during cooking. Cook the kebabs under a moderate heat, turning frequently, for 15–20 minutes or until evenly browned and cooked through.

Serves: 10
Preparation time: 15–20 minutes, plus marinating time
Cooking time: 15–20 minutes

450g (1lb) leg of mutton, fat trimmed off, minced

1 teaspoon crushed fresh green chillies

1 teaspoon garam masala

1 teaspoon chilli powder

1 teaspoon crushed garlic

1 teaspoon crushed fresh root ginger

2 medium onions, finely chopped

2 tablespoons chopped fresh coriander leaves and stalks

55g (2oz) plain flour or gram flour

per 100g	MED fat	MED saturated fat	LOW salt	LOW sugar
per portion (% of GDA)	87 kcal 4%	4g fat 6%	1.5g saturated fat 8%	0.0g salt 0%	1.5g sugars 2%

Meatball curry

Serves: 4
Preparation time: 10 minutes
Cooking time: 45–50 minutes

450g (1lb) lean minced lamb, beef
   or mutton
1 teaspoon crushed garlic
1 large onion, finely chopped
½ teaspoon coarsely ground
   black pepper
1 teaspoon garam masala
1 egg
1 teaspoon rapeseed oil
1 teaspoon cumin seeds
1 teaspoon crushed fresh root ginger
400g (14oz) tomatoes, chopped
1 tablespoon tomato purée
½ teaspoon turmeric
50–80ml (2–3fl oz) water (optional)
chopped fresh coriander (optional)

If you like your curries served with traditional flatbreads, leave out the extra water in this recipe. However, if you are a rice fan, add the water, which will result in a more liquid 'masala' (spicy gravy) for soaking into the rice.

1 Mix together the meat, garlic, half the onion, the black pepper, garam masala and egg in a bowl. Shape the meat mixture into 24 balls.

2 Preheat the grill on a medium setting. Line the bottom of a grill tray with foil and place the meatballs on a grill rack set over the grill tray. This will allow any fat to drain off while cooking. Grill the meatballs for 10–15 minutes or until nicely browned. Set aside.

3 Gently warm a pan, then pour in the rapeseed oil and add the cumin seeds and the remaining onion. Cook until the onion is soft, then stir in the ginger.

4 Add the chopped tomatoes, tomato purée and turmeric. Cook for 10 minutes.

5 Add the meatballs, reduce the heat and simmer for 20 minutes. If the sauce is looking too dry, add some water, a little at a time, to get the right consistency. Remove from the heat and garnish with chopped coriander, if using.

To freeze: Allow the dish to cool completely, then transfer to a rigid freezer-proof container. Cover, seal and label, and freeze for up to 1 month. To serve, defrost completely, then reheat thoroughly.

per 100g	MED fat	MED saturated fat	LOW salt	LOW sugar
per portion (% of GDA)	240 kcal 12%	11g fat 16%	5g saturated fat 13%	0.5g salt 8%	5g sugars 6%

Curry goat with ginger & sweet potato

Serves: 6
Preparation time: 15 minutes, plus marinating time
Cooking time: 1¾–2¼ hours

500g (1lb 2oz) lean goat meat or 750g (1lb 10oz) on the bone

2 tablespoons mild curry powder

4cm (1½in) piece of fresh root ginger, peeled and finely chopped

2 cloves garlic, finely chopped

1 large onion, finely chopped

4 pimento (allspice) berries, crushed

1 tablespoon sunflower oil

410g (14½oz) can chickpeas, rinsed and drained

1 red pepper, deseeded and sliced

Scotch bonnet pepper, to taste, sliced

1 large sweet potato, peeled and cubed

2 spring onions, thickly sliced

This is a celebratory West Indian dish, served at parties and family gatherings. You don't have to stick to goat – mutton or lamb work equally well. The slow cooking makes the meat deliciously tender. Serve curry goat with plain boiled rice and a green salad.

1 Wash the meat, remove any visible fat and cut it into bite-sized chunks. If using meat on the bone, remove any visible fat but leave the meat on the bone. Put the meat into a large bowl and add the curry powder, ginger, garlic, onion and pimento. Mix together, cover and leave the meat to marinate in the refrigerator overnight if possible, or for a few hours at least.

2 Using a Dutch pot or large pan, gently fry the remaining ingredients, except for the sweet potato and spring onion, for 3–5 minutes. Add the goat meat with all the marinade and stir well.

3 Add enough water to cover the meat and leave to simmer with the lid on for 1–1½ hours or until the water has reduced to a rich sauce. Add the sweet potato and cook for a further 40 minutes or until the meat is tender, adding the spring onions for the last 10 minutes of cooking time.

To freeze: Allow the dish to cool completely, then transfer to a rigid freezer-proof container. Cover, seal and label, and freeze for up to 1 month. To serve, defrost completely, then reheat thoroughly.

per 100g	LOW fat	LOW saturated fat	LOW salt	LOW sugar
per portion (% of GDA)	**220 kcal** 11%	**4.9g fat** 7%	**0.8g saturated fat** 4%	**0.5g salt** 8%	**2.7g sugars** 3%

Stir-fried ginger beef with peppers

Serves: 2
Preparation time: 20 minutes
Cooking time: 10–12 minutes

1 teaspoon cornflour

4 tablespoons water

1 tablespoon reduced-sodium
   soy sauce

1 teaspoon dark soft brown sugar

2–3 teaspoons sunflower oil

175g (6oz) lean rump or fillet steak,
   cut into thin strips across the grain

1½ teaspoons Sichuan pepper,
   crushed

1 small red pepper, deseeded and cut
   into strips

1 small green or yellow pepper,
   deseeded and cut into strips

1 carrot, peeled and cut into thin
   matchsticks

55g (2oz) mangetout, trimmed

4 spring onions, chopped

1 fresh red chilli, deseeded and finely
   chopped

2cm (⅔in) piece of fresh root ginger,
   peeled and cut into thin strips

1 clove garlic, finely chopped

This lightning-quick, tasty stir-fry is great for weekday suppers, and offers you an easy way to boost your five-a-day intake. Serve it with noodles or plain boiled rice.

1 In a small bowl, blend together the cornflour with the water until smooth. Stir in the soy sauce and sugar and set aside.

2 Heat 1 teaspoon of the sunflower oil in a wok. Add the beef and crushed pepper and stir-fry over a fairly high heat for 3–4 minutes or until the beef is browned all over. Using a slotted spoon, transfer the beef to a warm plate and set aside.

3 Carefully add the remaining oil to the hot juices in the wok. Heat the oil over a medium heat until hot, then add the peppers, carrot, mangetout, spring onions, chilli, ginger and garlic. Stir-fry over a medium-high heat for 3–5 minutes or until softened or cooked to your liking.

4 Return the beef and any juices to the wok and stir to mix. Add the cornflour mixture to the wok and stir-fry over a medium heat for 1–2 minutes or until the beef is hot. Serve immediately.

Variation: Try using lean pork or chicken breast instead of beef.

per 100g	LOW fat		LOW saturated fat		LOW salt		LOW sugar	
per portion (% of GDA)	303 kcal	15%	11g fat 16%	3.2g saturated fat 16%	1.3g salt 22%	15g sugars 17%		

Fish

DISHES

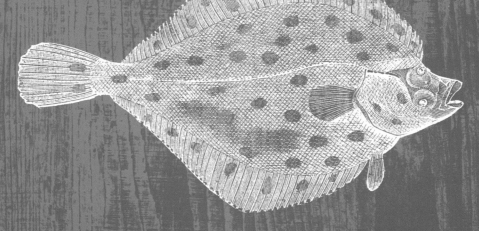

Bengali fish curry

Known as 'macher jhol' in Bengali, this fish-curry recipe features white fish fillets that are coated in spices and fried, before being cooked in a light, fresh and spicy fresh-tomato sauce. Serve this dish with plain Basmati rice, naan (see page 100) or chapatis (see page 99).

1 Mix together the turmeric, cumin, ground coriander, chillies and two-thirds of the coriander leaves. Coat the fish evenly with this mixture.

2 Heat 1 teaspoon of oil in a frying pan. Fry the fish for 2 minutes on each side or until lightly browned. Drain on kitchen paper and set aside.

3 Heat the remaining oil in the same pan and add the mustard and cumin seeds. When the mustard seeds pop, add the garlic, ginger, onion and tomato. Fry gently for 8 minutes. Add the boiling water and stir for 1 minute.

4 Return the fish to the pan and simmer for 10–12 minutes or until the sauce is brownish and not too thick, and the fish is cooked through. Garnish with the remaining coriander and serve hot.

To freeze: Allow the dish to cool completely, then transfer to a rigid freezer-proof container. Cover, seal and label, and freeze for up to 1 month. To serve, defrost completely, then reheat thoroughly.

Serves: 2
Preparation time: 5–10 minutes
Cooking time: 20–25 minutes

½ teaspoon turmeric

1 teaspoon ground cumin

1 teaspoon ground coriander

2 fresh green chillies, chopped

3 tablespoons chopped fresh coriander

500g (1lb 2oz) hoki or haddock fillets, skinned and cut into 7.5–9cm (3–3½in) long pieces

3 teaspoons rapeseed oil

½ teaspoon brown or black mustard seeds

¼ teaspoon cumin seeds

2 cloves garlic, crushed

1 teaspoon crushed fresh root ginger

1 medium onion, finely chopped

2 medium tomatoes, roughly chopped

200ml (7fl oz) boiling water

per 100g	LOW fat		LOW saturated fat		LOW salt		LOW sugar	
per portion (% of GDA)	324 kcal	16%	11.5g fat 16%	1.5g saturated fat 8%	0.6g salt	10%	6g sugars	7%

White fish masala curry

Serves: 6
Preparation time: 5–10 minutes, plus marinating time
Cooking time: 20–25 minutes

450g (1lb) white fish, such as cod or haddock

2 tablespoons lemon juice

2 teaspoons olive oil

1 medium onion, chopped

1 teaspoon crushed garlic

1 teaspoon crushed fresh root ginger

2 small tomatoes, liquidized or skinned and finely chopped

1 teaspoon cumin-coriander powder

1 teaspoon crushed fresh green chilli

½ teaspoon turmeric

½ teaspoon garam masala

1½ teaspoons ground black pepper

Use your favourite white fish to make this tasty dish, in which the fish is poached over a gentle heat in a flavoursome 'masala' (spicy gravy). This curry is great served with plain boiled rice or Indian flatbreads and a side dish of salad or vegetables.

1 Cut the fish into bite-sized chunks, sprinkle with the lemon juice and leave in the refrigerator for 10 minutes.

2 Heat the oil in a pan and fry the onion and garlic until soft, then add the ginger, tomato and all the spices and cook for about 5 minutes.

3 Add the fish. Ensure the sauce covers the fish completely. Add a little water to stop the fish from sticking to the pan, if necessary, and simmer over a low heat for 10–15 minutes until the fish is cooked through and the masala has penetrated the flesh.

Cook's tip: Fish is a nutritious choice, but it's important that we consider the environment and sustainability issues when buying it. Look out for on-pack information or talk to your fishmonger to help guide you.

per 100g	LOW fat	LOW saturated fat	LOW salt	LOW sugar
per portion (% of GDA)	87 kcal 4%	2g fat 3%	0.5g saturated fat 3%	0.1g salt 2%	2g sugars 2%

Spicy hilsa fish

Serves: 4
Preparation time: 10 minutes, plus marinating time
Cooking time: 15–20 minutes

450g (1lb) hilsa fish

1½ teaspoons turmeric

1 tablespoon rapeseed oil

1 medium onion, diced

1 teaspoon crushed fresh green
    chillies

3 whole fresh green chillies, slit
    lengthwise

1 teaspoon cumin-coriander powder

1 teaspoon English mustard powder
    (optional)

2 tablespoons finely chopped fresh
    coriander

The hilsa fish, also known as ilish in Bengali, is a highly favoured fish in India. It is prepared to celebrate festivities and mark religious occasions in many parts of the subcontinent. Hilsa fish is an oily fish, which means it contains omega 3 fats. Eat a portion per week of oily fish to help keep your heart healthy, or two to three portions if you have had a heart attack. Serve this dish with plain Basmati rice and a side dish of salad or vegetables.

1 Cut the fish into bite-sized pieces and rinse them under cold water. Use kitchen paper to blot the fish pieces dry, then rub the turmeric over the flesh and leave the fish in the refrigerator for 20 minutes.

2 Heat the oil in a pan, then add the diced onion, crushed chilli, whole chilli, cumin-coriander powder and mustard (if using) and sauté for 3 minutes. Turn off the heat and add the fish to the pan. Mix well until the fish pieces are well coated in the spiced oil.

3 Place a steamer dish over a pan of boiling water. Put the fish pieces into the steamer dish, replace the lid and steam for 10–15 minutes or until the fish is cooked. Remove the fish from the pan and garnish with the chopped coriander before serving.

Variation: Try using mackerel or salmon in place of the hilsa fish.

per 100g	**MED** fat		**LOW** saturated fat		**LOW** salt		**LOW** sugar	
per portion (% of GDA)	**339 kcal** 17%	**25g fat** 36%	**0.5g saturated fat** 3%		**0.2g salt** 3%		**1.5g sugars** 2%	

Five-spice fish

Panch phoran is a classic Bengali spice blend, made using cumin, mustard, fennel, nigella and fenugreek seeds. This refined flavour complements the fish wonderfully in this tempting recipe. Serve this dish with chapatis (see page 99) or plain Basmati rice and a side dish of salad or vegetables.

1 Cut several slits in the skin of the fish using a sharp knife, then rub in the turmeric all over the fish and into the slits.

2 Heat the oil in a frying pan and fry the fish for 2–3 minutes on each side until golden. Remove the fish from the pan with a slotted spoon and set aside.

3 In the same oil, fry the panch phoran and chillies for 1 minute.

4 Now return the fish to the pan. Add the boiling water. Cover and simmer for 5 minutes until the sauce has thickened and the fish is cooked.

Variation: Try using pollock or coley fillets in place of the sea bass.

Cook's tip: Panch phoran is an East Indian blend of 5 spices. It gives a distinctive flavour to vegetable and pulse dishes. It's usually tempered in hot oil or clarified butter before the other ingredients in the dish are added. To make panch phoran spice blend, mix 1 teaspoon fenugreek seeds, 1 teaspoon cumin seeds, 1 teaspoon fennel seeds, 1 teaspoon brown mustard seeds and 1 teaspoon nigella seeds, then roast them in a dry frying pan set over a medium heat for 2–3 minutes, until you can smell the aromas of the spices. Don't let the seeds burn. Allow to cool. Either leave the seeds whole, or grind them in an electric spice grinder or by using a pestle and mortar. Store the spice blend in an airtight container for up to 6 months. 1 teaspoon of whole or ground panch phoran can be used in a recipe to serve 4 people. To make a wet paste, mix 2 teaspoons of cold water with every teaspoon of ground panch phoran.

Serves: 2
Preparation time: 5–10 minutes
Cooking time: 12 minutes

400g (14oz) sea bass, gutted, scaled and washed
¼ teaspoon turmeric
1 tablespoon rapeseed oil
½ teaspoon panch phoran
2 fresh green chillies, slit lengthwise
150ml (¼ pint) boiling water

per 100g	MED fat	LOW saturated fat		LOW salt		LOW sugar	
per portion (% of GDA)	204 kcal 10%	9.5g fat 14%	1.5g saturated fat 8%	0.3g salt 5%	0g sugars 0%		

Steamed snapper

Serves: 4
Preparation time: 10 minutes, plus marinating time
Cooking time: 30 minutes

Scotch bonnet pepper, to taste, finely sliced (optional)

2 cloves garlic, crushed

½ teaspoon coarsely ground black pepper

1 bay leaf

½ teaspoon ground coriander

2 sprigs fresh thyme, leaves picked

2 pimento (allspice) berries, crushed

4 snapper fillets (each about 150g/5½oz)

200g (7oz) pumpkin, peeled, deseeded and cubed

150g (5½oz) okra, washed and trimmed

1 onion, thinly sliced

400g (14oz) can chopped tomatoes

This scrumptious West Indian dish of steamed 'snappa' is quick and easy to make, and is great served with boiled yams or plain boiled rice and vegetables of your choosing.

1 Mix together the Scotch bonnet pepper, garlic, black pepper, bay leaf, ground coriander, thyme and crushed pimentos and spread the mixture over the fish. This can be done in advance and left to marinate in the refrigerator overnight.

2 Put the vegetables in a large non-stick pan with a little water and heat gently for 5–7 minutes.

3 Place the marinated fish on top of the vegetables and cover with a tight-fitting lid. Simmer over a low heat for 20 minutes or until the fish is cooked all the way through. Serve immediately.

Cook's tip: Use another firm-fleshed white fish of your choice, such as coley or cod, in place of the snapper.

per 100g	LOW fat	LOW saturated fat	LOW salt	LOW sugar
per portion (% of GDA)	**220 kcal** 11%	**3.5g fat** 5%	**0.8g saturated fat** 4%	**0.4g salt** 7%	**3.6g sugars** 4%

Barbecued mackerel with spices

Serves: 2
Preparation time: 10 minutes
Cooking time: 10–12 minutes

1 teaspoon finely grated orange zest

1 tablespoon freshly squeezed
orange juice

2 teaspoons olive oil

1 teaspoon ground cumin

1 teaspoon ground coriander

½ teaspoon hot chilli powder

1 clove garlic, finely chopped

Freshly ground black pepper, to taste

2 whole fresh mackerel (each about
280–350g/10–12oz unprepared
weight), gutted and cleaned

Small orange wedges and chopped
fresh flat-leaf parsley, to garnish
(optional)

Spices work very well with the flavour of mackerel, which is also a great fish to barbecue. This spicy fish dish is not only healthy but delicious, too. Serve it with couscous or some nutty brown rice and a crisp green salad.

1 Light your barbecue about 30–45 minutes before you want to start cooking.

2 Combine the orange zest, orange juice, olive oil, ground spices, garlic and black pepper in a bowl and whisk together.

3 Make 3 deep cuts in each side of each fish. Rub the spice mixture over the fish and into the cuts.

4 Place the fish on the rack over the barbecue and cook for 5–6 minutes on each side or until the flesh is firm and opaque and the skin is slightly charred. Garnish with the orange wedges and fresh parsley, if using, to serve.

Cook's tip: When barbecuing, the coals are hot enough to begin cooking when they are glowing red and covered with a thin layer of white ash.

per 100g	MED fat	MED saturated fat	LOW salt	LOW sugar
per portion (% of GDA)	**384 kcal** 19%	**29.4g fat** 42%	**5.8g saturated fat** 29%	**0.3g salt** 5%	**0.6g sugars** 1%

Ackee & smoked mackerel

Ackee, the national fruit of Jamaica, has a lovely soft texture, similar to that of scrambled egg. It is often eaten as part of a main dish, accompanied by rice, yams, plantains or some type of dumpling. In this dish, the salty fish plays off the fruitiness of the ackee very well.

Serves: 8
Preparation time: 5 minutes
Cooking time: 10 minutes

1 tablespoon vegetable oil

1 red pepper, deseeded and finely sliced

1 large onion, finely sliced

Scotch bonnet pepper, to taste, finely sliced

2 cloves garlic, finely sliced

2 beef tomatoes, chopped

200g (7oz) can ackee, drained

Freshly ground black pepper, to taste

100g (3½oz) smoked mackerel, cut into bite-sized pieces

1 Heat the oil in a pan. Add the red pepper, onion, chilli and garlic and cook until the vegetables are tender.

2 Add the chopped tomato to the cooked vegetables, stirring very gently so as not to break up the tomato flesh. Cook for 3–5 minutes until the tomato is heated through.

3 Add the ackee, black pepper and mackerel and cook very gently for 1–3 minutes until piping hot. Serve immediately.

per 100g	MED fat	LOW saturated fat	LOW salt	LOW sugar
per portion (% of GDA)	120 kcal 6%	9.1g fat 13%	1g saturated fat 5%	0.48g salt 8%	3.6g sugars 4%

Grilled mackerel with sweet chilli & lime

Serves: 4
Preparation time: 10 minutes
Cooking time: approximately 30 minutes

500–600g (1lb 2oz–1lb 5oz) sweet potatoes, scrubbed and cut into chunky chips

Low-calorie cooking spray or 1 teaspoon unsaturated oil

Large pinch of chilli flakes

Freshly ground black pepper, to taste

Few sprigs fresh thyme, leaves picked

4 teaspoons Thai sweet chilli sauce

¼ teaspoon ground pimento (allspice)

Thumbnail-length of fresh root ginger, peeled and finely grated

Zest and juice of 1 large lime, plus lime wedges to serve

4 mackerel fillets (each about 150g/5½oz)

250g (9oz) green beans

In this dish, mackerel is coated in tropical flavours, such as lime, ginger and pimento, before being grilled, then served with roasted sweet potato wedges and lightly cooked green beans.

1 Preheat the oven to 180°C/fan 160°C/gas mark 4. Spread out the sweet potatoes on a baking tray, mist well with cooking spray or drizzle over the oil, and season with chilli flakes and black pepper. Bake for 15 minutes, then turn the potatoes, scatter over the thyme and cook for another 15 minutes or until they are golden and cooked through.

2 Meanwhile, preheat the grill on a high setting and mix together the chilli sauce, pimento, ginger and lime zest and juice. Smear this mixture over the flesh of the fish and place the fish, skin-side up, on a grill pan lined with foil. (You can cut the fillets in half if you like, for an attractive presentation.) Grill for 5–6 minutes until the skin is beginning to blister in places and the flesh is just opaque.

3 Meanwhile, cook the beans for 3–4 minutes in boiling water, then drain well. Serve with the fish, sweet potato wedges and extra lime for squeezing.

Cook's tip: Be careful not to overcook the fish or it will dry out. Cook until just opaque. Allow the fish to rest for a few minutes after cooking, wrapped up in the foil. The result will be perfectly cooked juicy flesh.

per 100g	HIGH fat		LOW saturated fat		LOW salt		LOW sugar	
per portion (% of GDA)	446 kcal 22%	22.3g fat 32%	4.5g saturated fat 23%		0.8g salt 13%		10.2g sugars 11%	

Grilled salmon

Serves: 4
Preparation time: 5–10 minutes, plus marinating time
Cooking time: 15–20 minutes

2 tablespoons lemon juice

½ teaspoon coarsely ground
    black pepper

½ teaspoon cumin-coriander powder

4 salmon steaks

2 teaspoons olive oil

1 medium onion, sliced

1 teaspoon finely chopped garlic

½ teaspoon finely chopped fresh
    root ginger

1 teaspoon crushed fresh green
    chillies

1 tablespoon finely chopped
    fresh coriander

These succulent salmon steaks suffused with Indian spices are special enough for entertaining, yet practical enough for a quick evening meal. Serve this dish as part of a buffet, or with some flatbread and a salad.

1 Mix the lemon juice, pepper and cumin-coriander powder in a small bowl. Spread this mixture on both sides of the salmon steaks. Place the steaks on a plate or in a bowl, cover and leave to marinate in the refrigerator for 1–2 hours.

2 Heat the oil in a frying pan and fry the onion until soft. Add the garlic, ginger and green chillies and continue to cook for 2 minutes. Preheat the grill on a medium setting.

3 Remove the onion mixture from the pan. Place the salmon steaks on non-stick baking paper on a grill tray, then spread the onion mixture on each side of the fish steaks. Grill for 15–20 minutes, turning the fish and basting it with the marinade occasionally.

4 Remove the salmon steaks from the grill tray and garnish with coriander before serving.

Cook's tip: This dish can also be cooked in the oven. After spreading the onion mixture over the fish, place it in an ovenproof dish, cover with foil and cook at 190°C/fan 170°C/gas mark 5 for 20–30 minutes.

per 100g	MED fat		MED saturated fat		LOW salt		LOW sugar	
per portion (% of GDA)	**281 kcal**	14%	**17g fat** 24%	**3g saturated fat**	15%	**0.16g salt**	3%	**1.5g sugars** 2%

Masala prawns

Known as 'bhuna jhinga', this relatively dry prawn curry is delicious and very quick to make with mostly store-cupboard ingredients. Serve it with flatbreads such as paratha, naan (see page 100) or chapatis (see page 99) and a side dish of salad or vegetables.

1 Shell the prawns and remove the fine black thread that runs along their backs. Wash the prawns thoroughly.

2 Heat the oil in a pan, then add the cumin and onion and cook until the onion is soft and just brown at the edges.

3 Add the garlic and chillies and half of the chopped coriander and cook the mixture for 1 minute.

4 Add the prawns, cumin-coriander powder, yoghurt and a little water, if necessary, and simmer for 5 minutes or until the prawns are cooked.

5 Remove the pan from the heat, garnish the dish with the remaining coriander and serve immediately.

Cook's tip: For a stronger curry flavour, add 1 teaspoon of finely grated fresh root ginger and 1 teaspoon of crushed fresh green chillies.

Serves: 6
Preparation time: 15 minutes
Cooking time: 10 minutes

450g (1lb) fresh or frozen and thawed large uncooked prawns
2 teaspoons rapeseed oil
1 teaspoon cumin seeds
1 small onion, chopped
4–5 cloves garlic, finely chopped
1–2 fresh green chillies, thinly sliced
1 tablespoon finely chopped fresh coriander
1 teaspoon cumin-coriander powder
1 tablespoon low-fat natural yoghurt

per 100g	LOW fat	LOW saturated fat	LOW salt	LOW sugar
per portion (% of GDA)	51 kcal 3%	1.6g fat 2%	0.1g saturated fat 1%	0.18g salt 3%	0.9g sugars 1%

Jamaican jerk marinade with prawns

Serves: 4
Preparation time: 15 minutes, plus marinating time
Cooking time: varies, depending on the size of the prawns used

200g (7oz) peeled uncooked prawns
Lime wedges to serve (optional)

For the jerk marinade:
2.5cm (1in) piece of fresh root ginger, peeled
4 spring onions, roughly chopped
2 teaspoons pimento (allspice) berries, crushed using a pestle and mortar
1–2 Scotch bonnet peppers, or to taste
3 cloves garlic
1 tablespoon brown sugar
1 teaspoon ground black pepper
1 teaspoon mixed spice
2–3 fresh thyme sprigs, leaves picked, plus extra leaves to garnish
3 tablespoons olive or rapeseed oil
Zest and juice of 1 lime, plus extra zest to garnish

Jerk seasoning is very popular spice from Jamaica and is a favourite for barbecues, but ready-made seasoning can be high in salt. In this homemade version, flavours like ginger, lemon and thyme make this prawn dish delicious without the need for added salt. Serve the prawns with a bowl of plain boiled rice mixed with chopped coriander and chopped green spring onion tops.

1 If you are using bamboo skewers, soak them in cold water for 30 minutes before threading the prawns onto them.

2 First make the marinade. Using a hand blender or food processor, blend the ginger, spring onions, crushed pimento, Scotch bonnet, garlic, sugar, pepper, mixed spice and thyme to a smooth paste, then mix in the oil and lime juice.

3 Thread the prawns onto the skewers, then rub the marinade over them. Place the skewers on a platter, cover and marinate in the refrigerator for 1 hour.

4 Preheat the grill on a medium setting. Grill the prawns, turning regularly, until cooked through. About 2–3 minutes before the end of the cooking time, scatter over some thyme leaves and lime zest. Serve immediately, with lime wedges, if using.

Variation: You can use this marinade to make jerk chicken. To feed 4, use about 1.3kg (3lb) oven-ready chicken. Remove the skin and cut the chicken into quarters. Add a tablespoon of rum to the marinade, if desired, and rub it over the chicken. Marinate the chicken, covered, for at least 4 hours, or overnight, preferably, then cook on the barbecue or on a baking sheet in a preheated oven at 180°C/fan 160°C/gas mark 4 for about 45 minutes or until the chicken is thoroughly cooked and very tender. Jerk chicken is excellent served with Rice and Peas (see page 92).

per 100g	MED fat		LOW saturated fat		LOW salt		LOW sugar	
per portion (% of GDA)	124 kcal	6%	8.2g fat 12%	0.6g saturated fat 3%	0.3g salt 5%	3.3g sugars 4%		

Vegetarian
DISHES

Spiced tofu & carrot burgers

These grilled veggie burgers make a delicious change to meat and will be enjoyed by vegetarians and meat lovers alike. Serve them with a salad of crispy leaves and crunchy cucumber, or in buns with all the usual trimmings, like slices of tomato and a tasty relish or chutney.

1 Heat 2 teaspoons of the olive oil in a small pan set over a medium-high heat. Add the shallots or onion, carrots and garlic and cook for 4 minutes or until softened, stirring frequently. Add the ground spices and cook for 1 minute, stirring.

2 Transfer the shallot mixture to a bowl. Add the tofu, breadcrumbs, cheese, tomato purée and chopped coriander and season with black pepper. Mix well using a fork, then use your hands to press or gently squeeze the mixture together to bind it.

3 Preheat the grill on a medium setting. Shape the mixture into 4 large (jumbo) or 6 smaller round flat burgers (each about 2.5cm/1in thick). Lightly brush each burger all over with the remaining olive oil.

4 Place the burgers on a wire rack in a grill pan and grill, turning once, for about 10–15 minutes or until the burgers are lightly browned and cooked.

Variation: Use ground almonds in place of the breadcrumbs.

Serves: 2–4 (makes 4–6 burgers)
Preparation time: 35 minutes
Cooking time: 10–15 minutes

4 teaspoons olive oil

6 small shallots or 1 onion, finely chopped

175g (6oz) carrots, peeled and coarsely grated

1 clove garlic, crushed

1½ teaspoons ground coriander

1½ teaspoons ground cumin

1 teaspoon hot chilli powder

350g (12oz) firm tofu, drained and mashed

55g (2oz) fresh wholemeal breadcrumbs

55g (2oz) reduced-fat mature Cheddar-type cheese, finely grated

2 tablespoons tomato purée

1 tablespoon chopped fresh coriander

Freshly ground black pepper, to taste

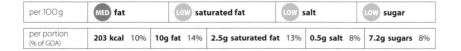

per 100g	**MED** fat		**LOW** saturated fat		**LOW** salt		**LOW** sugar	
per portion (% of GDA)	**203 kcal** 10%	**10g fat** 14%	**2.5g saturated fat** 13%		**0.5g salt** 8%		**7.2g sugars** 8%	

Chunky vegetable chilli

Serves: 6
Preparation time: 10 minutes
Cooking time: about 1½ hours

2 teaspoons sunflower oil

1 onion, chopped

1 green or red pepper, deseeded and diced

2 cloves garlic, crushed

1 large fresh green chilli, deseeded and finely chopped

2 teaspoons ground cumin

1 teaspoon hot chilli powder

400g (14oz) can chopped tomatoes

1 tablespoon tomato purée

3 carrots, peeled and diced

175g (6oz) swede, peeled and diced

175g (6oz) mushrooms, wiped clean and sliced

3 sticks celery, finely chopped

250ml (9fl oz) homemade vegetable stock (see page 13) or low-salt ready-made vegetable stock

Freshly ground black pepper, to taste

420g (15oz) can red kidney beans, rinsed and drained

Chopped fresh coriander, to garnish

This delicious vegetarian chilli is a great winter warmer. Serve it with brown or white rice, a small portion of homemade guacamole and a little low-fat natural yoghurt.

1 Preheat the oven to 180°C/fan 160°C/gas mark 4. Heat the oil in a large flameproof, ovenproof casserole dish on the hob, then add the onion, pepper, garlic and green chilli and sauté for 5 minutes or until softened.

2 Add the cumin and chilli powder and cook gently for 1 minute, stirring. Stir in the tomatoes, tomato purée, carrots, swede, mushrooms, celery, stock and black pepper.

3 Bring to boil, then cover, transfer the casserole dish to the oven and cook for 1 hour, stirring once. Then stir in kidney beans, cover again and cook in oven for a further 20–30 minutes or until the vegetables are tender. Garnish with chopped coriander to serve.

To freeze: Allow the dish to cool completely, then transfer to a rigid freezer-proof container. Cover, seal and label, and freeze for up to 1 month. To serve, defrost completely, then reheat thoroughly.

per 100g	LOW fat		LOW saturated fat		LOW salt		LOW sugar	
per portion (% of GDA)	**138 kcal** 7%	**2.6g fat** 4%	**0.3g saturated fat** 2%		**0.75g salt** 13%		**10.1g sugars** 11%	

Yam & gungo soup

Serves: 6
Preparation time: 10 minutes
Cooking time: 50 minutes

2 litres (3½ pints) water

400g (14oz) can pigeon peas

400g (14oz) yams, peeled and
    chopped into medium-sized pieces

2 cloves garlic, finely chopped

4 spring onions, finely chopped

1 large green pepper, deseeded and
    cut into bite-sized pieces

1 Scotch bonnet pepper or fresh red
    chilli, or to taste, finely chopped

3 sprigs fresh thyme

6 pimento (allspice) berries, finely
    chopped

fresh thyme leaves to garnish
    (optional)

This spicy West Indian recipe combines yam with pigeon peas (gungo) for a tasty soup. The yam provides a filling starchy carbohydrate, while the pigeon peas are a good source of protein.

1 Bring the water to the boil, then boil the peas and yams for about 20 minutes until they are almost cooked.

2 Add all the other ingredients and simmer for about 30 minutes until the broth thickens. Serve warm, garnished with fresh thyme leaves, if using.

Variation: Use potato as a substitute for yam. Try using canned red kidney beans or black-eyed beans in place of the pigeon peas.

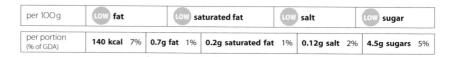

per 100g	LOW fat	LOW saturated fat	LOW salt	LOW sugar
per portion (% of GDA)	**140 kcal** 7%	**0.7g fat** 1% **0.2g saturated fat** 1%	**0.12g salt** 2%	**4.5g sugars** 5%

Bitter melon (karela) curry

Serves: 5
Preparation time: 10 minutes, plus standing time
Cooking time: 10–15 minutes

175g (6oz) karela

1 tablespoon lemon juice

1 tablespoon olive oil

1 teaspoon cumin seeds

1 medium onion, chopped

1 tablespoon amchur or 1 cooking apple, peeled and chopped

1 tablespoon chopped coriander leaves and stalks

½ green pepper, deseeded and sliced

55g (2oz) cabbage, sliced

½ teaspoon turmeric

1 teaspoon garam masala

1 teaspoon ground cumin

2 teaspoons crushed fresh green chillies

Also known as 'karela' in Hindi, bitter melon is similar in size and shape to a cucumber, but with a knobbly skin. It has a distinctive, grown-up flavour – a tasty, highly savoury bitterness that is wonderfully showcased in this dish. Serve this curry with chapatis (see page 99).

1 Peel and wash the karela and cut them into 5mm (¼in) slices. Toss them in lemon juice and leave to stand for 1 hour.

2 Squeeze the karela slices and discard the bitter juice from them.

3 In a heated pan, add the oil and cumin seeds and cook for 1 minute.

4 Add the karela to the hot oil and cook for 2–3 minutes on each side or until just brown.

5 Add the remaining ingredients and cook over a low heat for 7–10 minutes or until the cabbage is cooked.

per 100g	LOW fat	LOW saturated fat	LOW salt	LOW sugar
per portion (% of GDA)	**60 kcal** 3%	**3g fat** 4%	**0.5g saturated fat** 3%	**0g salt** 0%	**5g sugars** 6%

Potato curry

This is a great everyday curry, ideal for quick after-work suppers and weekend lunches, and for when comfort food is called for. Serve it with plain Basmati rice, chapatis (see page 99), naan (see page 100) or pitta bread.

1 Boil the potatoes, unpeeled, for 10–15 minutes. Allow them to cool, then peel and slice them in half.

2 Heat a pan over a medium heat, then add the oil. Once this is warm, add the cumin and mustard seeds. When the seeds start to pop, put in the asafoetida, garlic, tomatoes and spices and cook for 5 minutes.

3 Add the potatoes, then bring the mixture to the boil. One boiled, let it simmer gently for 3–4 minutes.

4 Remove the pan from the heat and stir in the lemon juice. Garnish the curry with chopped coriander and serve immediately.

Serves: 6
Preparation time: 10 minutes
Cooking time: 20–30 minutes

225g (8oz) small red potatoes or new white potatoes
1 tablespoon olive oil
1 teaspoon cumin seeds
1 teaspoon mustard seeds
½ teaspoon asafoetida
1 teaspoon crushed garlic
225g (8oz) tomatoes, liquidized
½ teaspoon chilli powder or crushed fresh green chillies
1 teaspoon cumin-coriander powder
½ teaspoon turmeric
1 teaspoon lemon juice
1 tablespoon chopped fresh coriander to garnish

per 100g	MED fat		LOW saturated fat		LOW salt		LOW sugar	
per portion (% of GDA)	66 kcal	3%	3g fat 4%	0.5g saturated fat 3%	0.11g salt	2%	1g sugars	1%

Okra curry

Serves: 6
Preparation time: 5–10 minutes
Cooking time: 15–20 minutes

450g (1lb) okra

1 tablespoon olive oil

1 teaspoon cumin seeds

2 medium onions, chopped

1 teaspoon crushed fresh green chillies

1½ teaspoons cumin-coriander powder

½ teaspoon turmeric

½ tablespoon chopped fresh coriander stalks

1 medium tomato, chopped

½ tablespoon chopped fresh coriander leaves to garnish

1 tablespoon lemon juice (optional)

Okra, known as 'bindi' or 'bhinda' in some Indian dialects, is naturally low in sodium and low in saturated fat, counts towards your five-a-day and has an interesting texture and flavour. When buying okra, look for small pods, which are the most tender, and ensure the skin is nice and fresh, not dry looking. If a pod snaps when bent, it is fresh. Serve this dish with chapatis (see page 99) or naan (see page 100).

1 Rinse the okra pods under cold running water. (There's no need to dry them.) Cut them into pieces that are 1–2.5cm (½–1in) long. Set aside.

2 Heat the oil in a large pan, then add the cumin seeds and chopped onion and cook over a medium heat until the onions are soft.

3 Add the okra, green chilli, cumin-coriander powder, turmeric and chopped coriander stalks. Mix well.

4 Add the tomato and cook, uncovered, for 5 minutes over a medium heat. Reduce the heat to low and cook for 7–10 minutes or until the okra is tender, stirring every 2–3 minutes.

5 Remove the pan from the heat and place the okra mixture in a serving dish. Garnish with the chopped coriander leaves and sprinkle over the lemon juice, if using, just before serving.

per 100g	LOW fat		LOW saturated fat		LOW salt		LOW sugar	
per portion (% of GDA)	65 kcal	3%	3g fat	4%	0.5g saturated fat	3%	0.03g salt	1%	4.5g sugars	5%

Aubergine & potatoes in tomato sauce

Serves: 2
Preparation time: 5–7 minutes
Cooking time: 15–20 minutes

2 medium dried red chillies

1 tablespoon coriander seeds

1 teaspoon cumin seeds

1 teaspoon brown or black mustard seeds

3 teaspoons rapeseed oil

1 medium onion, thickly sliced

½ teaspoon turmeric

2 bay leaves (optional)

300g (10½oz) white or red potatoes, cut into 2cm (¾in) cubes

300g (10½oz) aubergine, cut into 2.5cm (1in) cubes

2 cloves garlic, crushed

1 medium tomato, finely chopped

1 teaspoon tamarind concentrate

400ml (14fl oz) boiling water

Tamarind adds a delicious lemony citrus note to the flavour of this dish. You can buy it as a concentrate or paste in Asian shops or online. Serve this curry with plain Basmati rice and dhal or homemade naan (see page 100).

1 In an electric spice grinder, or using a pestle and mortar, grind the chillies, coriander, cumin and mustard seeds to a powder. Set aside.

2 Heat the oil in a large pan, then add the onion, turmeric and bay leaves (if using). Fry over a medium heat for 2–3 minutes.

3 Add the potatoes and fry for 1 minute. Cover and cook for 7 minutes over a medium heat until the potatoes are tender. Half way through cooking, check that the potatoes are not sticking to the bottom of the pan. Dislodge them with a wooden spoon if they are.

4 Add the aubergine and garlic and fry for 1 minute.

5 Add the tomato and fry for another minute, then cover and cook for 6 minutes. Stir in the ground spices and tamarind concentrate.

6 Add the boiling water, then cover and cook for 10 minutes, stirring half way through cooking. Serve immediately.

per 100g	LOW fat	LOW saturated fat	LOW salt	LOW sugar
per portion (% of GDA)	289 kcal 14% · 8.7g fat 12%	0.7g saturated fat 4%	0.1g salt 2%	12.6g sugars 14%

Mutter 'paneer'

Serves: 6
Preparation time: 5 minutes
Cooking time: 20–25 minutes

300g (10½oz) firm tofu

2 tablespoons rapeseed oil

½ teaspoon mustard seeds

½ teaspoon cumin seeds

1 small onion, chopped

2 medium tomatoes, chopped

1 teaspoon tomato purée

1 teaspoon cumin-coriander powder

1 tablespoon chopped fresh
   coriander

½ teaspoon chilli powder

½ teaspoon turmeric

100ml (3½fl oz) water

450g (1lb) frozen peas

Mutter paneer is a classic North Indian curry made with peas and paneer cheese. In this version, the paneer is replaced with tofu – the two are similar in texture and they both have the useful characteristic of taking on the flavours of the spices they are cooked with. However, paneer is high in saturated fat, so tofu makes the perfect substitute in this 'fusion-food' take on a well-loved dish.

1 Cut the tofu into 2cm (¾in) cubes. Set aside.

2 Warm a large pan over a medium heat, then add the oil. When the oil has warmed slightly, put in the mustard and cumin seeds. Once the seeds begin to pop, add the onion and cook until soft.

3 Put in the tomato, tomato purée and all the spices and cook for 5 minutes.

4 Add the tofu pieces to the pan with the water. Bring to the boil, then add the peas. Reduce the heat and simmer for 10 minutes. Serve warm.

Cook's tip: Because standard paneer is high in saturated fat, you might find that tofu is a good alternative in many dishes. While 100g (3½oz) of paneer has 18g of saturated fat, the same amount of tofu has less than 1g on average.

per 100g	**MED** fat	**LOW** saturated fat	**LOW** salt	**LOW** sugar
per portion (% of GDA)	**134 kcal** 7%	**7g fat** 10% **1g saturated fat** 5%	**0.03g salt** 1%	**4g sugars** 4%

Curried green bananas

Serves: 4
Preparation time: 5 minutes
Cooking time: 35 minutes

5 green bananas

2 tablespoons mustard oil

1 large onion, finely chopped

1 tablespoon finely chopped fresh
    root ginger

1 teaspoon turmeric

1 level teaspoon chilli powder

2 cardamom pods, crushed

Scotch bonnet pepper, finely
    chopped, to taste, plus extra,
    sliced, to garnish (optional)

225ml (8fl oz) water

225ml (8fl oz) natural yoghurt

1 teaspoon garam masala

Green bananas are more firm in texture than regular bananas, and their flavour is similar to that of potato or yam. They can be found in West Indian, African or Asian shops. Serve this delicious dish with plain boiled rice and a side dish of salad or vegetables for an interesting alternative curry for the family.

1 Make an incision along the length of each banana. This will make it easier to peel the bananas once they are cooked. Add the bananas to a pan of boiling water and cook for about 15 minutes, until the flesh can be easily pierced with a fork. Once cooked, remove the skins and slice the flesh into 2cm (¾in) discs. Set aside.

2 Heat the oil in a large pan. Fry the onion and ginger for 2–3 minutes, then add the turmeric, chilli powder, cardamom pods and Scotch bonnet. Cook everything for about 1 minute.

3 Stir the banana slices into the onion-and-spice mixture and allow them to brown slightly. Now add the water, mix well, then cover and cook gently for 15 minutes. Finally, stir in the yoghurt and garam masala and heat through gently for a further minute. Don't overheat the mixture or the yoghurt will curdle. Serve immediately, garnished with the Scotch bonnet slices, if using.

per 100g	LOW fat	LOW saturated fat	LOW salt	LOW sugar
per portion (% of GDA)	**200 kcal** 10% | **2.8g fat** 4%	**0.6g saturated fat** 3%	**0.2g salt** 3%	**8.1g sugars** 9%

Sweet potato curry with spinach & chickpeas

Serves: 2
Preparation time: 15 minutes
Cooking time: 25 minutes

1 sweet potato (about 250g/9oz unprepared weight), peeled and cut into small chunks

2 teaspoons sunflower oil

1 small red onion, chopped

1 clove garlic, crushed

1 fresh red chilli, deseeded and finely chopped

1cm (½in) piece of fresh root ginger, peeled and finely chopped

1 teaspoon medium or hot curry powder, or to taste

½ teaspoon ground cumin

½ teaspoon turmeric

227g (8oz) can chopped tomatoes

100ml (3½fl oz) vegetable stock (preferably homemade – see page 13)

210g (7½oz) can chickpeas, drained and rinsed

115g (4oz) fresh baby spinach leaves, rinsed and drained

1 tablespoon chopped fresh coriander (optional)

This sweet-savoury curry is delicious, quick and easy to make, and full of goodness. The warming spices and fresh, healthy ingredients combine to produce a tempting supper. Serve with brown or white Basmati rice.

1 Cook the sweet potato chunks in a pan of boiling water for about 7 minutes or until tender. Drain well and set aside.

2 Heat the sunflower oil in a non-stick pan, then add the onion and cook gently for about 5 minutes or until softened. Now add the garlic, chilli and ginger and cook gently for 3 minutes, stirring occasionally. Stir in the ground spices and cook gently for a further minute, stirring.

3 Stir in the tomatoes, stock, chickpeas and sweet potato chunks. Bring to the boil, then reduce the heat and simmer for 5 minutes, stirring occasionally. Stir in the spinach, cover the pan with a lid and cook gently for 2–3 minutes or until the spinach has wilted. Take the pan off the heat and stir in the coriander, if using, just before serving.

per 100g	LOW fat	LOW saturated fat	LOW salt	LOW sugar
per portion (% of GDA)	319 kcal 16%	7g fat 10% 0.8g saturated fat 4%	0.5g salt 8%	14.3g sugars 16%

Vegetable biriyani

Serves: 6
Preparation time: 15 minutes
Cooking time: 20–25 minutes

1 small carrot, peeled and cut into small cubes

1 medium potato, peeled and cut into small cubes

25g (1oz) green pepper (about ¼ pepper), deseeded and diced

25g (1oz) red pepper (about ¼ pepper), deseeded and diced

25g (1oz) French beans, finely chopped

50g (1¾oz) frozen peas

1 teaspoon tomato purée

½ teaspoon finely chopped fresh green chillies

1 teaspoon garam masala

¼ teaspoon turmeric

550g (1lb 4oz) cooked Basmati rice

1 small onion, finely chopped

4 roasted cashew nuts, chopped

½ teaspoon roasted cumin seeds

½ teaspoon chilli powder

This healthy dish is perfect as the main course for a celebratory vegetarian meal. It is wonderfully fragrant and very delicious. It's also surprisingly simple to make, which is an added bonus.

1 Preheat the oven to 160°C/fan 140°C/gas mark 3. Cook the carrot, potato, peppers, French beans and peas in a pan of boiling water for 3–4 minutes or until tender. Drain and return the vegetables to the pan.

2 Add the tomato purée, green chillies, garam masala and turmeric to the vegetables and mix well.

3 Place half the cooked rice at the bottom of an ovenproof dish, spread the vegetable mixture on top, then arrange the rest of the rice on top of the vegetables, distributing it evenly. Sprinkle the top layer of rice with the chopped onion, cashew nuts, roasted cumin seeds and chilli powder.

4 Cover the dish with foil and cook the rice-and-vegetable mixture in the preheated oven for 15 minutes. Alternatively, the rice can be mixed with the cooked vegetables just before serving.

Variations: To make a meat biriyani, use 550g (1lb 4oz) diced lean lamb, beef or chicken. Place the meat in a pan with about 400ml (14fl oz) water, the tomato purée, green chillies, garam masala and turmeric and cook over a medium-high heat for about 10 minutes, adding extra water if necessary to prevent the meat sticking to the pan. When the meat is cooked through, proceed with layering the meat mixture and rice and cooking in the oven as directed in steps 3 and 4 above.

per 100g	LOW fat	LOW saturated fat	LOW salt	LOW sugar
per portion (% of GDA)	**161 kcal** 8%	**1.1g fat** 2%	**0g saturated fat** 0%	**0.03g salt** 1%	**1.9g sugars** 2%

Rice & peas

Serves: 6 as a main meal, 10 as a side dish
Preparation time: 5 minutes, plus soaking time
Cooking time: 2–2½ hours

250g (9oz) dried red peas or red kidney beans

350ml (12fl oz) homemade vegetable stock (see page 13)

6 spring onions, chopped

2 sprigs fresh thyme

Freshly ground black pepper, to taste

400g (14oz) long-grain white rice

1 whole Scotch bonnet pepper or 1 fresh red chilli

A favourite in the West Indies, many a Jamaican or Barbadian meal can boast this dish as a cornerstone. Serve rice and peas on its own, or reduce the quantities and serve it with grilled chicken or fish and some vegetables.

1 Put the peas or beans in a bowl, cover with cold water and soak them overnight.

2 Drain the peas or beans, place them in a large, heavy-based saucepan and add enough water to cover them. Bring to the boil and boil rapidly for 10 minutes. Drain and discard the water.

3 Return the peas or beans to the pan and cover with fresh water. Bring to the boil, then reduce the heat, cover and simmer for 1¼–1½ hours or until the peas or beans are tender. Drain well.

4 Rinse out the pan, then return the cooked peas or beans to the pan. Add the vegetable stock, spring onions, thyme, black pepper and rice to the pan. Now top it up with water – there should be about 2½ times as much liquid as there are rice and peas.

5 Place the whole Scotch bonnet pepper or the red chilli on top and bring to the boil. Reduce the heat, cover and simmer for about 25–30 minutes or until all of the liquid has been absorbed and the rice is tender. Do not stir while cooking or allow the Scotch bonnet pepper or chilli to burst!

6 Remove and discard the Scotch bonnet pepper or chilli and the thyme sprigs. Lightly fluff up the rice and peas using fork, and serve.

Variations: Use dried pigeon peas or dried garden peas in place of the kidney beans. Pigeon peas, also known as gungo, are the more traditional choice.
Cook's tip: Add 2 crushed cloves of garlic and 1 cinnamon stick with the spring onions, if desired. Remove and discard cinnamon stick before serving.

per 100g	LOW fat	LOW saturated fat	LOW salt	LOW sugar
per portion (% of GDA)	**370 kcal** 19%	**3.1g fat** 4%	**0.7g saturated fat** 4%	**0.1g salt** 2%	**1.3g sugars** 1%

Mung bean curry

Mung beans are considered cleansing and cooling in many Eastern traditions. Their soluble fibre content may help to reduce cholesterol. Serve this delicious curry with plain Basmati rice and a side dish of salad or vegetables.

Serves: 8
Preparation time: 10 minutes
Cooking time: 20–30 minutes

225g (8oz) whole mung beans
600ml (1 pint) water
1 small onion, roughly chopped
1 medium tomato
2 fresh green chillies
1 teaspoon crushed fresh root ginger
½ teaspoon crushed garlic
3 whole cloves
1 teaspoon cumin seeds
2 cinnamon sticks (each about 2.5cm/1in long)
1 teaspoon garam masala
1 teaspoon coriander-cumin powder
½ teaspoon chilli powder
½ teaspoon turmeric
1 teaspoon lime juice
1 tablespoon chopped fresh coriander stalks and leaves

1   Wash the mung, then put them in a pressure cooker with the water. Cover with the pressure-cooker lid and cook over a high heat for 5 minutes.

2   Meanwhile, liquidize the onion, tomato, green chillies, ginger and garlic, then add the liquidized mixture to the mung beans in the pressure cooker. Cover and cook for 5–10 minutes, until the beans are soft and mushy.

3   Dry-roast the cloves, cumin seeds and cinnamon sticks together in a dry frying pan, then grind the roasted spices to a fine powder using a pestle and mortar or in an electric spice grinder. Add this powder, with the other spices, to the mung beans and continue to cook over a medium heat for about 5 minutes, until the pressure cooker's whistle blows.

4   When the whistle blows, depressurize and remove the lid. Reduce the heat to low and cook for a further 5–10 minutes (depending on how well cooked you like your dhal). Remove the pressure cooker from the hob and stir in the lime juice and chopped coriander leaves and stalks just before serving.

Cook's tips: If you don't have a pressure cooker, put the washed mung beans in a saucepan with 850ml (1½ pints) water and bring to the boil, then simmer for 30–40 minutes until the beans are split and soft. Add the liquidized mixture from step 2 and cook over a low heat for 10 minutes, then add the spices and cook for a further 5–10 minutes to allow the spices to infuse the dish, and until the beans are cooked to your liking. You can prepare brown lentils (whole masoor) using the same recipe and either of the cooking methods given here.

per 100g	LOW fat	LOW saturated fat	LOW salt	LOW sugar
per portion (% of GDA)	**97 kcal** 5% **0.8g fat** 1%	**0g saturated fat** 0%	**0.03g salt** 1%	**1.3g sugars** 1%

Breads

& CHUTNEYS

Khasta roti

Serves: 10
Preparation time: 10 minutes, plus rising time
Cooking time: 10–15 minutes

500g (1lb 2oz) wholemeal flour, plus extra for dusting
2 teaspoons caster sugar
1 teaspoon ajowan seeds
300ml (½ pint) cold water

'Khasta' means crispy, crumbly and flaky in Hindi, and this oven-baked whole-wheat bread has a satisfying crunch. It is a crisp alternative to the other, softer, Indian flatbreads in this book.

1 Sift the flour into a bowl and stir in the caster sugar, ajowan seeds and cold water. Knead for 10 minutes into a firm dough. Place the dough in a bowl, cover with a damp cloth and leave to stand in a warm place for 15 minutes.

2 Preheat the oven to 180°C/fan 160°C/gas mark 4. Divide the dough into 10 equal balls. Dust your work surface with flour and roll out each ball into a circle that measures about 10cm (4in) across.

3 Prick each dough circle evenly across the surface with a fork, then place them on a baking tray and bake for 8–10 minutes, in batches if necessary, until light brown and slightly bubbly on the surface.

per 100g	MED fat	LOW saturated fat	LOW salt	LOW sugar
per portion (% of GDA)	**216 kcal** 11%	**4.1g fat** 6%	**0.4g saturated fat** 2%	**0.02g salt** 0%	**2.1g sugars** 2%

Red chutney

Serves: 15
Preparation time: 5 minutes
Cooking time: none

1 red pepper, deseeded and cut into chunks
4–5 hot fresh red chillies, deseeded and thickly sliced
1 teaspoon lemon juice
1 tablespoon water
1 teaspoon ground cumin
Pinch of asafoetida

This spicy chutney made with red pepper and red chilli is great with kebabs (see page 49), pakoras or any barbecued meat.

1 Put all the ingredients into the bowl of a blender and liquidize until smooth. Store the chutney in a glass jar in the refrigerator for up to 4 days.

Variations: Try adding either 2 cloves of garlic or 100g (3½oz) strawberries. If you add strawberries, don't add the tablespoon of water.

per 100g	LOW fat	LOW saturated fat	LOW salt	MED sugar
per portion (% of GDA)	**5 kcal** 0.25%	**0.1g fat** 0%	**0g saturated fat** 0%	**0g salt** 0%	**0.7g sugars** 1%

Green chutney

Serves: 8
Preparation time: 5 minutes
Cooking time: none

1 green pepper, deseeded and cut into chunks
6 hot fresh green chillies, deseeded and thickly sliced
4 tablespoons chopped fresh coriander leaves
4 tablespoons chopped fresh coriander stalks
1 tablespoon lemon juice
1 tablespoon water
½ teaspoon ground cumin

Perfect with grilled fish and meat, this coriander and green pepper chutney is also good with pakoras and kebabs.

1 Put all the ingredients into the bowl of a blender and liquidize until smooth. Store the chutney in a glass jar in the refrigerator for up to 4 days.

Variations: Use 1 small raw mango or 1 cooking apple in place of the lemon juice.

Cook's tip: You can add onion or fresh mint to this mixture. To retain the fresh green colour of this chutney, serve on the day you make it.

per 100g	LOW fat	LOW saturated fat	LOW salt	LOW sugar
per portion (% of GDA)	**5 kcal** 0.25%	**0.2g fat** 0%	**0g saturated fat** 0%	**0.01g salt** 0%	**0.5g sugars** 1%

Potato raitha

Serves: 8
Preparation time: 5 minutes
Cooking time: 15 minutes (to cook the potatoes)

300ml (½ pint) low-fat natural yoghurt

175g (6oz) new potatoes, boiled and cut into small cubes

¼ teaspoon coarsely ground black pepper

½ teaspoon cumin seeds, roasted

1 small onion, finely chopped

1 tablespoon finely chopped fresh coriander

½ teaspoon roasted and ground cumin seeds

½ teaspoon chilli powder

½ teaspoon crushed fresh green chilli

Raitha is a seasoned yoghurt relish that's a popular and cooling accompaniment to Indian food. This refreshing raitha is very easy to make and works well with most curries and rice dishes, such as pilau (see page 39) and meat or vegetable biriyani (see page 90) and with barbecued meat or fish.

1 Whisk the yoghurt until smooth.

2 Add the potatoes, black pepper, cumin seeds, onion and half the coriander. Mix well.

3 Place in a serving dish and garnish the top with the remaining coriander, the ground roasted cumin, chilli powder and the green chilli.

per 100g	LOW fat	LOW saturated fat	LOW salt	LOW sugar
per portion (% of GDA)	40 kcal 2%	0.5g fat 1%	0g saturated fat 0%	0.1g salt 2%	3g sugars 3%

Index

Acknowledgements

The British Heart Foundation would like to thank Seroj Shah, Charlene Shoneye, Manju Malhi, Anne Sheasby and Lizzie Harris for their recipes.

Simon & Schuster Illustrated would like to thank the British Heart Foundation for their help and support.

Picture credit:

The Eatwell Plate on page 8 is © Crown copyright material and appears courtesy of the Department of Health in association with the Welsh Government, the Scottish Government and the Food Standards Agency in Northern Ireland.